WATER FEATURES
for Small Gardens

From Concept to Construction

KEITH DAVITT

TIMBER PRESS

Published in 2003 by
Timber Press, Inc.
The Haseltine Building
133 S.W. Second Avenue, Suite 450
Portland, Oregon 97204, U.S.A.
www.timberpress.com

For contact information regarding editorial, marketing, sales, and distribution in the
United Kingdom, see www.timberpress.co.uk.

Reprinted 2006

Printed through Colorcraft Ltd., Hong Kong

Library of Congress Cataloging-in-Publication Data

Davitt, Keith.
    Water features for small gardens : from concept to construction / by Keith Davitt.
        p. cm.
    Includes bibliographical references and index.
    ISBN-13: 978-0-88192-596-8
    ISBN-10: 0-88192-596-9
        1. Water gardens. 2. Fountains. 3. Water in landscape architecture. I. Title.

SB423.D39 2003
714—cd21   2003047309

A catalog record for this book is also available from the British Library.

CONTENTS

PREFACE

IN MY TWENTY YEARS of designing and building landscapes I have found no single feature more effective in bringing charm and grace, beauty and magic to a garden than a water feature. This is especially true for small gardens. Where else can you find placid calm and eternal movement melded into a shimmering display of brilliant color and caressing sound, dancing light and performing life forms that bring you so much daily pleasure—all in a few square feet? Water gardens have a quality of brightness and of life, they provide a sense of immediacy, and they tend to pull you into the moment and into their interiors in a way few other elements can.

Water gardens also add value to your home. A well-designed and well-constructed water feature is special. It gives another dimension to the garden and sets it off as a place more extraordinary than others, more unique, and, consequently, more desirable.

Contrary to what many people still think, water gardens are not the finicky, time consuming things of infinite demand they once were. Even ponds, the most demanding of the various water features, require far less work than a lawn or perennial border. But, you ask, what about mosquitoes? Fish (and the movement of water) prevent any mosquitoes from being in the water garden. I do not mean there will be fewer mosquitoes or that there will usually be none; I mean that with only one fish there will never be any mosquitoes!

Developments through the 1990s in construction materials have made water gardens relatively easy and inexpensive to install. No matter how small an area you have, there is a water feature that will turn that space into a place more wonderful to be in and to see.

The purpose of this book is threefold: to help you decide which water feature is right for you and the style of garden you have or wish to have; to illuminate principles of design for water features in intimate spaces; and to provide complete information on how to build the water feature of your choice. I will show you how to successfully incorporate each type of water feature into an existing landscape and how to design a landscape that includes a water feature as a natural and embellishing component. Rather than approach this in a theoretical sense, I draw upon specific projects, examining both the design considerations and the construction details. Twenty years of building water features has given me considerable opportunity for making most of the possible mistakes, so a good helping of "what not to do" is sprinkled throughout the sections on building water features.

The water features shown in this book are, for the most part, not difficult or expensive to create. Too many water-feature books depict astonishing examples of elaborate water features that are beyond the reach of most people in terms of difficulty, amount of space needed, and expense. Most of the ponds, streams, and fountains depicted here were built by just a couple of people. With a little time and careful attention to detail, the features are within the capabilities and budgets of most homeowners. I have presented exceptions only to demonstrate specific points.

You might find it helpful to peruse the book, noting those gardens and water features that particularly please you. If you find a water feature that you like and think would look good in your garden, or if you see a kind of garden you would like to have on your property, study that project and then refer to the chapter on constructing that kind of water feature. Otherwise, just carry on reading, as in the next section we take a general look at the various types of water features and the settings they are suited for. After that, we go into details on particular projects. Each chapter on a given type of water feature is followed by construction details for that particular feature. Somewhere within these pages you will likely find a water feature perfectly suited to your tastes and garden.

Which Water Feature?

NATURAL POOLS, raised pools, raised and in-ground fountains, wall fountains, streams, bog gardens, water-filled, planted and stocked wine barrels, and waterfalls—what they all have in common is that they each contain water and, with the exception of the bog garden, recirculate the water in ornamental display by means of a hidden, usually submersible pump. Each can be a considerable asset in the right location, and one or more of these features is probably right for you and your garden. In this chapter I describe what each of these water features is, and in the remaining chapters we look at specific water feature projects and the environments they occupy.

1. Natural Pools

The natural pool is the most commonly built water feature and what most people envision when they think of a fishpond. Natural pools are in-ground constructions, built of flexible or rigid liners, but they can be made with concrete as well. They are "free-form" in shape, although in city gardens, where space is very limited, they may be made to conform to some specific area. The natural pool can be a couple of feet across or can occupy an entire landscape. Water is recirculated by means of a submersible pump, often entering the pool after a short run over rocks or via a gentle or dramatic waterfall. Stones, plants, and small animals complete the picture.

The natural pond is made to look as if nature put it there and is often the most suitable water feature for many urban and suburban landscapes. Most gardens are informal in layout, and the natural pool can easily be incorporated into these gardens as a harmonious component. However, as you will see, many fine design possibilities suit the informal landscape, and other styles of landscapes can also include a natural pool. If the layout of your garden or the garden you want to have is free-form and the environment you wish to create is to have the feeling and mood of a natural world, then the informal or natural pool is the best for you. Your planting would also be informal, at least in the immediate vicinity of the water garden, and you may want to consider including a stream and or waterfall as well.

2. Raised, Informal Pools

The informal, raised pool differs from the natural pool in that it is above grade and does not necessarily attempt to represent nature. It is different from the formal fountain only in shape as it is not symmetrical. However, its construction is often identical with that of the formal fountain. Water usually enters the informal, raised pool as a visible stream or controlled fall, contributing both visually and audibly to the beauty of the pool.

There are many situations in which raised, informal pools are the most suitable sorts of water features. For example, if your garden is not symmetrical in layout and contains an irregular retaining wall, a raised pool might work well somewhere behind the wall. A raised, informal pool may also be suitable for many contemporary gardens that may be curvilinear or geometric but are asymmetrical in layout. Planting around the informal raised pool can vary considerably from the completely informal and loose to the tightly controlled with clipped hedges or topiary, for example. If your garden is relaxed in feel but for whatever reason does not lend itself to an in-ground pool, the raised, informal pool may be just the solution.

3. Raised, Formal Fountains

Formal fountains are symmetrical in shape and either raised or in the ground. The in-ground fountain is the simplest formal fountain to build. Raised, formal fountains tend to be more dramatic than in-ground fountains, providing more of an architectural element. In-ground, formal fountains, on the other hand, frequently have a serene quality about them.

4. In-ground, Formal Fountains

A raised, formal fountain is significantly different in construction from an in-ground water feature. Generally, it is more difficult to build and thus requires more skill, is more costly both materials and labor, and can be a little more difficult to maintain. That said, the above-ground formal fountain can be just the right element for a given setting and provide as much pleasure and beauty as any pond or stream. A formal fountain is symmetrical in shape, though the shape can be quite complex, as in, for example, a fountain in a Moorish design. Water jets or a central fountain usually displays the water in action.

If your garden is a classical or formal landscape characterized by symmetry and balance with clearly defined and organized spaces and would profit from an architectural element, then the formal water garden is appropriate. Such a feature would likely be best situated centrally along at least one axis and possibly as the focal point of the garden. The very rear of the garden can make an ideal location, particularly in a small landscape, and if there is a rear wall, you might consider a wall fountain with water falling into a raised, formal pool.

The construction of the in-ground, formal fountain is much like that of the natural pool in that an excavation is made water retentive by a liner or other non-permeable material. The primary difference is that an in-ground, formal pool must be excavated to exact dimensions to achieve the desired effect. There are water garden suppliers who will construct a perfectly square or rectangular liner according to your specifications as well as provide the necessary hardware to secure the corners in place.

The in-ground, formal water feature serves the same aesthetic function as the raised, formal pool but provides less of an architectural element. It is often a focal or axial point in the landscape and usually displays water in motion through water jets or a fountain. Sometimes the in-ground water feature is intended primarily as a display for water lilies, lotuses, and other such aquatics. You will often see this kind of water feature as part of a botanic garden. In the home landscape, it is usually part of a symmetrical garden arrangement and is also usually the focal point. Though the water will be below or nearly at ground level, there may be an edging of stone or concrete accentuating the pool's shape.

If you wish to display aquatic flora in a dramatic arrangement or if your garden is characterized by symmetry and balance, by right angles or cross axes, and contains sculpture or other classically formal elements, then the in-ground, formal water garden will serve you well.

5. Wall Fountains

Wall fountains are normally quite simple and are characterized by being self-contained with the fountain and basin joined into a single construction. Aside from the bog garden, the simplest wall fountain is the easiest water feature to install. Many very handsome, self-contained units simply need to be mounted against a wall with a power source nearby. For example, you may have a lion's head with a stream of water that flows from its mouth into a small basin beneath it in which sits the pump that recirculates the water back to the spout. The electric cord goes through the back of the mount just above or at water level to an outlet. Though very simple, wall fountains add a wonderfully elegant touch to a garden wall and garden, providing the quiet sound and soothing sight of water in motion. Both formal and informal landscapes lend themselves to the wall fountain, provided there is—or can be—a wall. Many urban landscapes are candidates for this type of water feature because they nearly always have a wall in close proximity to the garden.

6. Streams

A stream is, well, a stream. Water runs visibly down a watercourse from either a pool or waterfall to a pool and from which it is then pumped back, unseen, to the upper source. Constructing the stream is much the same as constructing a natural pool; in fact, a stream can be thought of as a shallow, elongated pool. Streams can be built of masonry, of fiberglass liners, or, more commonly, of flexible liners.

Though not often considered viable in small gardens, streams are, in my view, among the most delightful elements almost any sized garden can contain. Fifteen linear feet is sufficient for quite a dramatic watercourse, and if done well, it will provide endless pleasure.

As with the bog garden and natural pool, a stream is at home in the informal landscape. If there is enough space, however, you will see that a stream can be the heart of a natural garden within a larger and not necessarily natural layout.

7. Bog Gardens

Sounds unappealing, doesn't it, a bog in your garden? Kind of like a pitfall or a bees' nest. The bog is probably the least considered of all possible water features, but if you enjoy wetland plants and want to grow unusual and unusually beautiful plants that cannot be cultivated any other way, or if you have a naturally boggy area, then a bog garden may be just the thing.

A bog garden is built much as the natural pool is, with a water-retentive liner providing a continuously moist soil. It can be a stand-alone feature or a part of the "natural" pool or pond with water flowing into it from the pond. A naturally damp area in the garden can often be quite easily converted to a bog, and with proper planting, it will bring freshness and the quality of a true—and truly unusual—garden to a difficult site.

The considerations for the suitability of a bog garden are pretty much the same as for a natural pool in that a bog is usually given a natural layout and is used for cultivating or even naturalizing plants in a distinctly non-formal setting. If your landscape is informal and you want to cultivate exotic wetland plants, then a bog will suit you perfectly.

8. Tub Gardens

If you have a postage stamp of a garden or, even more suitably, a dot of a patio, or if you want to make a pleasant and uncommon statement at your front entrance, in your atrium, or on your deck, or if you have a small area where you simply cannot plant anything but would like to host a water feature, then consider the tub garden. Generally the size of a wine or whiskey barrel (in fact, tubs are often made from these barrels but are cut in half), the tub garden will occupy about three square feet of your available space. Within those three feet, however, you could have fish, water snails, a water lily, water poppies, ornamental grasses, and several other water plants. Water can emerge in a fountain, flow from a rock, shoot from the mouth of an ornament, or just sit in the tub supporting this world of flora and fauna. You can build your own tub garden using any of a variety of pots, tubs, or basins. You can also purchase kits that contain everything you need to complete a tub garden, including the flora and fauna. If your available space is really small, the tub garden is your ticket to the world of water.

9. Natural Waterfalls

I treat waterfalls as a separate item only because they are such an important component of many pools, fountains, and streams. Construction details are covered in the appropriate chapter, but a few general concepts are in order here.

Waterfalls can be really wonderful components of streams, fountains, and pools if tastefully done. However, most waterfalls we see in home water features are fairly sorry affairs for a variety of reasons having to do with material selection, size of the fall, and volume of the water. I discuss this concept extensively in various case studies and in chapter 9, Construction Details for Waterfalls. Let it be said here that a well-designed, well-constructed waterfall can be a thing of beauty, but unless proper technique is used, the result will be quite unsatisfying.

If you want the drama of falling water and have a setting that can support a contemporary structural element or if you have a pool or stream that can be enhanced by a waterfall, designing and constructing this feature will be well worth the effort.

PUMPS

Most water-garden pumps are designed for underwater placement. They are measured in terms of the number of gallons of water per hour they can deliver, and this can range from about fifty to several thousand. Most home water gardens use something between three hundred and fifty and twelve hundred gallons per hour, with five hundred to seven hundred and fifty gallons per hour being the most common for relatively small ponds. Of course, pump size depends on the size of the pond; a big pond needs a big pump.

Most suppliers of water-garden equipment are prepared to determine the size pump you need based on the volume of your pond and the distance of the water's travel and rise. The basic premise is that the entire volume of water should be recirculated at least once every two hours. To determine the water volume in gallons, measure the average width, the average depth, and the average length of the pond. Multiply this figure by seven and a half (the number of gallons of water per cubic foot), and you have a close enough measure of the gallons of water your pond holds. If that gallon amount is, say, seven hundred, then a five-hundred-gallon-per-hour pump is adequate, even allowing for pressure loss from hose friction and the upward distance the water must be moved. However, it is generally best to purchase a slightly larger pump, as you can easily restrict the output of the pump without harm by a simple flow-control valve, such as a gate valve on the return hose.

There are several manufacturers of pumps, and most pumps are very reliable. The primary difference in the pumps, apart from the flow rate, is whether one is energy efficient or not. Energy-efficient pumps are more expensive to purchase but less expensive to run. As they tend to last a long time, long-term economics favors this option.

Another kind of pump suited for larger ponds where a considerable flow is wanted can handle solids. Pumping from twelve hundred to several thousand gallons per hour, these pumps are not affected by leaf fall or debris up to one inch across. Filtration may still be necessary, however, to keep out smaller sediment that can cloud the pool. The stream and pools shown in the project that created A Wild, Romantic Ruins with a Stream Running Through uses this type of pump with no other filtration, and the water there is beautifully filtered.

FILTRATION

This discussion of filtration applies to all formal and informal in-ground and above-ground pools. Most purveyors of water-garden supplies recommend using a pre-filter and a mechanical or mechanical-biological filter. A mechanical filter prevents debris from reaching the pump but usually does not screen out very fine sediment. A biological filter also filters out debris and sediment while providing a medium in which beneficial bacteria may colonize. A mechanical-biological filter provides separate mechanical and biological filtration. Frequency of cleaning depends on the filter used. Many suppliers also offer a skimmer in place of the pre-filter. A pre-filter is a sponge or fiber-filter material through which the water passes on its way into the pump, which filters out large debris and sediment. It must be rinsed out regularly. A skimmer draws off surface debris and collects it into a bag that must be regularly emptied.

Numerous pre-filter systems are available and as many mechanical and biological filters, some of which include waterfall filters, carbon canister filters, vortex and bead filters for koi ponds, and ultraviolet (UV) sterilizers for destroying algae. Each system requires a different design and space allotment, and each requires different considerations for making it both accessible and well disguised. An entire industry has grown up around pond filtration, and new designs are offered each year. Much of this elaboration in filter offerings is extravagant and unnecessary for natural pools as a well-made and properly stocked pond requires very little filtration. After all, these are not swimming pools; they're natural habitats so the water should not be crystal clear. However, greater filtration may be necessary for formal or raised pools or for raising koi. Here we take a closer look at this potentially confusing subject.

MORE OR LESS?

Avoid overkill. Small ponds usually require small pumps, both in terms of functionality and aesthetics. Although a lot of water pouring into the small pond may be dramatic, such a sight will never look—or feel—right. Just as the garden with its water feature must be seen as a whole, so too must the water garden itself, and each of its components must be in scale not only with each other but also with the whole.

Bio-filters are redundant, at least as far as generating helpful bacteria in the natural pond is concerned. With the introduction of water plants and various fauna, helpful bacteria will in time colonize between and on the stones, in the pots, on the sides, and the bottom of the pots. You can't keep bacteria out, so there is no need to specially provide for them. That said, most authorities recommend a bio-filter. The argument is that it guarantees colonization of helpful bacteria, provides the cleanest water, which may be helpful in resisting fish diseases, and is the most thorough filtration possible.

Pre-filters of the types usually offered (sponges or layers of fibrous material) keep the water suitably clean. Many filters require frequent rinsing, but new models are now available that make cleaning fairly easy. Carbon canister filters are supposed to purify and remove toxins from the water, but since the water should not be perfectly pure, they may be unnecessary. Unless you want an unusual quantity of fish in your pond (for example, if you are raising koi), toxins are not a problem either. Algae zappers, which are pre-filters that use ultraviolet light to kill the algae, are likewise unnecessary. Bacteria are part of a natural, balanced ecosystem, and with the right flora and fauna in place, helpful algae will grow, and fish, snails, and especially floating and submersible plants will keep the undesirable algae in check.

If you are going to raise a large amount of fish, however, you will need the vortex, bead, or other filtration system designed for removing large quantities of waste. This is not the case with most home pools, however, and you can have up to fifteen or twenty fish in a six-foot by four-foot pond without an elaborate filtration.

Perhaps one of the best and simplest filtration systems for the average home pond consists of a fine mesh plastic basket, which may also be used with a pump-sock. The pump-sock is a nylon bag of finer mesh than the basket into which the pump is inserted. The pump-sock comes with a fiber-mesh liner that you may decide not to use, as it requires frequent cleaning. The liner is easy to remove, however, so it may be worth using. The pump is placed in the sock and they are then placed in the plastic mesh basket. If there tends to be sediment (from runoff, for example) or abundant leaf-fall, I recommend using the sock in addition to the basket, either with or without the fiber mesh. If there is not much runoff sediment, the mesh basket is filtration enough and requires only infrequent rinsing out. All these materials are available from pond equipment suppliers.

When you are choosing which filter to use, whether it's a bio-filter with mechanical filtration or something simpler, I advise that you sort through the catalog offerings and make your best guess based on the factors I've outlined. Every year more is available than the year before.

1

Natural Pools

Site condition

As the before image shows, this was an existing landscape that was quite overgrown, with a planted porcelain sink occupying place of prominence. The owner had for years thought about putting a small fishpond in but had always hesitated: would it destroy his existing landscape? would it be too expensive? was a water garden really feasible on his twenty feet by twenty feet of urban backyard? would it create a mosquito problem? and could he keep koi?

Yes to the koi, no to the mosquitoes, yes to a water garden being feasible on a plot that size, and no to it being costly or adversely affecting his existing landscape.

A perusal of his property showed that a natural pool was, just from a design point of view, an excellent idea. The garden had a wonderfully random collection of plants in splendid disarray, but it lacked a focal point and, because of this it lacked interest. There was a lot of attractive foliage and some flowers, but there was nowhere the eye wanted to settle. An elevated wood deck about four and a half feet above grade was the primary outdoor living space and was also the vantage point from which the garden was viewed.

Site design

The owner had lived with his garden for many years and, apart from the disorderliness of it all, he liked it. Such a riot of nature in the heart of a city does have its own charm and can certainly provide a welcome contrast to the harsh cityscape. To disregard what was here would have been both insensitive and wasteful. There was a reality—a theme—already in place, so rather than discard it all and begin from scratch, the jungly nature of the site was allowed to generate the motif for the garden. The water garden would in turn arise out of that garden and play a key role in it.

Water feature design

Normally, a garden will contain a patio and planting, perhaps an outdoor grill, a table, and chairs. These features and pieces of furniture nearly always necessitate putting the water garden to the side or rear of the garden, leav-

BEFORE:

An urban jungle in need of some organization.

ing sufficient space for outdoor living. Here, however, that restriction didn't apply, and since the garden was meant to be seen and not used, the pool could go just about anywhere, even in the garden's center.

A small koi pond, essentially round in shape, and small waterfall were designed and placed right in the middle of the garden, the most prominent spot. The intent was to create a pool as one might come upon it in a clearing in a dense woods with a small rivulet running into it. A pathway skirts the pond, which is edged in stone and planted in naturalizing perennials, ground covers, and overhanging shrubs. The occasional annual is tucked in here and there for seasonal color.

Note that stones not only edge the pond but also completely cover the interior of the pond and create islands within it. Placement is an important aspect in creating a natural water feature. Too often a "natural" pond is built with appropriate rock around its perimeter, but the moment you look into the pond, the illusion of naturalness is destroyed by a visible liner, a pump, a filter, and other artificial objects.

The new design called for a centrally placed water garden with plantings and a narrow walk all around.

A pool in a clearing in the forest.

It was important that the pond not be made too large in relation to the rest of the property, particularly because it was to go in the center of the garden. Not only was it desirable to have access all the way around the pool, but it also needed to be kept to the proper scale. Had it been placed in the far corner, for example, the apparent size of the rest of the garden would have been larger, making a larger pool more appropriate. With the pool in the center, it is viewed in relation to each of the various planting areas created around it between the pond and the four boundaries of the garden. This arrangement required a slightly smaller pool. However, the pond's smaller size is more than compensated for by its central, prominent position, which consequently makes it more enjoyable than it would have been anywhere else in the garden.

Another important consideration was the shape of the pool. Normally it is desirable to lay out the natural pond in an irregular form with the longest axis of the pond running through the longest axis of the garden. In other words, you create a natural layout making the best use of the available space. Here, however, the planting made the garden seem round, not axial, so the pond was given a roundish shape. This shape contributed to the harmony between the pool and its surroundings, helping to integrate it with the environment.

Several elements are worth noting about the waterfall for this garden: its size and height, the nature of its construction, its placement, and the volume of water flowing through it. Let's first look at placement.

It is always desirable and generally possible to create the illusion that the water in a natural pool has a natural source. The usual way of creating this effect is to construct a slight elevation in the vicinity of the waterfall and to densely clothe it in plants so that the water appears to flow from a slight embankment into a declivity or natural basin. This is exactly the formation that often occurs in nature: water moving through or over the earth at a higher elevation, emerging from the face of an embankment, and then falling into a pool that was formed by the continuous falling of water.

After the pond was built and was functional (construction details appear in the next chapter) but before all the stone was in place, the waterfall was constructed at the rear of the pond. Water emerging from the invisible interior of these plantings would provide the most convincing illusion of its "source" coming from some wandering stream. Such a placement would also offer the greatest visibility from the deck, and the sound of the falling water would be slightly amplified across the pool toward the deck.

The waterfall in this garden was made small in keeping with the size of the pond, but it was not so small as to be difficult to see from the deck. Note that the waterfall itself is quite simple. The water appears from some unseen source beneath a larger rock and flows over only two smaller rocks. These two smaller rocks are both tilted slightly forward and the bottom one has an angled face and thin lip so that the water flows off rather than under it (see chapter 9). Various other rocks were placed all around to help enhance the natural look. The log that sits atop the fall actually fell from a neighboring *Ailanthus altissima*, and as it fit right in, there it stayed.

SITE DETERMINES DESIGN

Preconceived notions and personal preferences can easily get in the way of appropriate design, and all too often do. In this instance, had the designer or the owner possessed a predilection for, say, a formal water feature, a jarring conflict could have resulted unless the entire landscape was changed into something in which a formal water garden would be appropriate. The design of the water feature needs to arise out of the style, feeling, and flavor of the setting it is to occupy if a pleasing and harmonious unity of place is to be created.

BIG IS GOOD, SCALE IS BETTER

Among the most important considerations when building a pond is its size. Often the tendency is to make it too large, the driving thought behind this being that the larger the pond, the more fish, water plants, and so on that can be accommodated. And this is true, but it is important to remember that a pond is part of a landscape, and if it detracts from the whole, it diminishes the overall affect because of the poor proportions and bad spatial relationships. Neither the garden nor the pond will be seen to advantage.

Similarly, a pond must not be made too small. An arbitrary preference for a particular size should not be what determines the size of the pond. Rather, its placement in the larger scene must dictate its dimensions.

PROPER PROPORTIONS BETWEEN WATERFALL AND POND

The size of a waterfall must always be in proportion to the size of the pond it feeds and to the amount of water flowing through it. A waterfall should only be big if it carries a lot of water and feeds a large pond. In nature, a large flow of water into a small pond will either create an overflow or a stream that flows out of the pond. A small pond needs a waterfall of a size where the volume of water entering the pond is in proportion to the size of the pond and the volume of water flowing over the waterfall is in proportion to the size of the waterfall

CREATE TRANSITIONS BETWEEN THE FALL AND SURROUNDINGS

When building waterfalls, remember that in nature they occur where rocks are an abundant element within the entire landscape. They are found not only in the fall but also above, below, and on both sides of the fall and stream. A waterfall that is a collection of stones with water running down them but that has no stones on either side looks completely contrived and should be avoided when designing the natural pond.

The waterfall was placed on the far side of the pool where it would look most natural and have the greatest impact.

Planting

Much of the existing shrubbery was pruned and thinned but kept in place. These provided a mature, full-grown look at the outset. Note in particular the forsythia and aucuba in the rear left overhanging the pond. Other shrubs and perennials were added to provide more of the wild look. The oak-leaf hydrangea (*Hydrangea quercifolia*) to the right of the waterfall has a wonderful pagan quality to it, as does the *Taxus baccata* 'Repandens' in the foreground, the mahonia (*Mahonia aquifolium*) to the right of the pond, and the ferns distributed about. Various spreading, upright, and floating water plants complete the picture.

The existing natural, junglelike quality of this environment was the theme around which the garden and water garden were developed. The site called for a completely natural, small pool deep enough to provide a home for overwintering fish. The pond and waterfall were built in proportion to each other and to the dimensions of the site, and the pond was placed centrally for maximum enjoyment from the primary outdoor living area. The pond was given a natural shape and was lined on both the inside and outside with stones.

We kept the existing plantings as much as possible but pruned and thinned them, and we incorporated other plants that had the right, "wild" feel to them. A path around one side of the pond was created for easy access to the pond without it infringing overly on the natural environment. Stepping stones lead to the path and pond.

Water in the Rockaways, a New York Neighborhood

Site condition

The situation here is very different from the last. Whereas the previous garden was well endowed with an unmistakable theme, this small front yard needed a complete transformation and gave no hint of the motif upon which the new garden could be built—except, perhaps, a reversal of the existing rigidity and a break with the suburban stereotype. This concept, along with the owners' wish for "lush abundance" generated the motif upon which the new garden would be built. For these reasons we agreed that a water feature would be a delightful contribution to the garden.

Water features are normally situated in more remote portions of a property, not in the front yard for a variety of reasons. The front yard is open to outside traffic—visiting pets or other animals, children at play, and so on. Water attracts like nothing else, so the water feature, which the owner very definitely wanted, had to be removed from the street's easy access and view; it also needed to be placed where it could be enjoyed by the owners.

Site design

As this was to be an entirely new garden, it was possible (and, in fact, necessary) to design the garden and the water feature as a unified whole. The tall porch that dominated the front yard needed to be masked and visually lowered. We also wanted to break out of the static, linear paradigm so typical of suburban landscapes with their rectangular lawns, straight walks, and rigid planting beds. Both these objectives—obtaining a sense of unity and moving away from the typical suburban landscape—could be achieved by terracing.

Two curving walls were built, so creating three planes from the existing lawn level to the level of the porch. These two walls produced a variety of positive results. First, they reduced the size of the lawn, allowing for more and varied planting, and they gave a curving line to the lawn, which further disburdened the site of that static quality. The terraces provided an abundance of planting beds of a graceful form, and the curves of the walls themselves were gracefully pleasant. Finally, building the walls generated the perfect place for the pond. In fact, the upper terrace, screened from the roadside yet easily visible from the house, was designed as the location the water gardens

BEFORE:

A static, suburban yard in need of transformation.

The water garden is behind the upper-most plantings, adjacent to the porch, and visible from the house.

would occupy. Placed here, the feature would be visible and audible upon entry into the house and could be enjoyed from within while being completely screened from the street side.

Water feature design

This naturalistic water garden, consisting of an upper pool flowing into a lower, was designed as a focal point for the top terrace, where it would be visible from the living room and upon entering and leaving the home. The water flows from a small fall that is elevated about twelve inches or so above the surface of the upper pond. Within this upper pool there is a small weir that allows the water to flow through and down several inches into the lower pond. Water flowing over the weir adds movement and interest while also helping to oxygenate the water, something the fish appreciate. The pools were given a natural, free-form shape and were edged and lined in river flats (smooth, flat rocks) and river rounds (smooth, round, water-worn rocks). Ledges that are built into the pool during construction serve as planting shelves and also allow for easy placement of stone.

A rich planting and sculpture enhance the setting.

Planting

The plantings around the pool screen out views to the street and serve as a backdrop to the water gardens. From the street it is not possible to know this water garden exists, yet framed as it is by a wealth of shrubs and perennials, the pond is nicely visible from the porch and home, with a pleasing backdrop behind and around it. The Japanese umbrella pine (*Sciadopitys verticillata*) is especially effective at screening out unwanted views year round. *Miscanthus sinensis* screens out the neighborhood while providing a graceful backdrop to the water, as do the rhododendron and the various clematis vines that clamber up vertical supports.

The density of plantings around the water garden helps create a little world in which the water garden is a natural element. Without those plantings, the water garden would seem out of place as it would be seen against the backdrop of the suburban neighborhood. Notice the role of sculpture here. This much foliage calls out for the solidity of structural elements, which is found here in the two bird sculptures. These two birds step out of the foliage, both of them blending and balancing perfectly with the abundant leafiness.

This site was a complete redesign, allowing perfect integration of the water feature with the setting it was designed to inhabit. The motif for the garden and the water garden was lush abundance in a naturalistic setting. The intent was to break out of the typical suburban paradigm and create a garden replete with graceful motion, abundant planting, and a secret pond tucked into its own corner and visible only from inside the house or upon entering and leaving it.

The fish pool was built in two parts. A waterfall flows into the upper pool and then into a lower pool through a small weir. The waterfall is high enough to provide substantial visual and audio impact without overpowering the pool it flows into.

The pools were given a dense planting, both to screen out the surrounding neighborhood and to create a proper setting for a natural pool. The pool itself is planted abundantly and blends well into the environment around it.

INTEGRATE THE WATER FEATURE WITH ITS SURROUNDINGS

Too often we see well-made water features, particularly of the natural style, situated so that they look completely contrived and out of place. This effect often results from the failure to integrate the water feature with its surroundings. If stones are used in the water garden, then some should also occur in its vicinity, and there should always be, particularly in this style, an abundance of plants. The plants within the water will unite visually with the margin plants, which in turn will blend with the surrounding landscape to create a natural transition from the water garden into the landscape.

In contemporary or formal designs, different elements will be used to unify the water feature with the environment in which it is found. For example, a formal, in-ground pool will not be found in a rustic setting, and a contemporary design will contain and be surrounded by contemporary materials contemporarily rendered.

A two-level water garden with waterfall cascading into the upper level and a weir in the lower level.

A Pool in the Woods

A natural pool in a rock basin.
Photo by John Glover.

Site condition

This little corner of the garden lent itself perfectly to becoming a natural pond. The ground fell slightly toward a natural depression, creating elevation changes that could be utilized and enhanced.

Site design

To make the pool look natural when completed, it was necessary that an abundant planting establish the native habitat in which a pond would be found. Large stones were brought in and placed to secure the sloping terrain and to simulate a natural outcropping. The outer areas were planted with larger shrubs, and the areas immediately around the pool were planted with small shrubs and perennials. This type of planting creates a natural transition from the woodsy background to the pool.

Water feature design

Several factors contribute to this being among the best-designed and well-built natural pools that can be created. The shape seems completely natural and is very satisfying with its undulant shoreline. The stones are perfect: although they are not river stone, they are completely convincing because they rise above the water and contain it within their massive solidity. They also look quite pleasing against the backdrop of water and are the perfect accompaniment to plants. The contrast between the foliage and the stone highlights the delicate quality of the plants and the strength of the stones, while the rich textural qualities of both the stones and the plants harmonize beautifully. Junipers never look as good as when they're in a setting such as this.

Planting

There are too many plants in this garden to list, but a few of the more prominent are the cotoneaster, juniper, taxus, hibiscus, weigela, and chamaecyparis. Also featured are a variety of perennials such as hostas, irises, ferns, and aquatic plants.

A particularly beautiful small pond edged with large stones and harmoniously planted rests like a rough jewel in a woodsy setting.

A Tranquil Pool by a Peaceful Patio

Site condition

Before redesign, this tiny space was devoid of pleasing elements and burdened with those that were disagreeable. The chain-link fence gave the place a prisonlike quality, the ubiquitous ivy (*Hedera*) was depressingly invasive, and the raised platform was purposeless. The small concrete patio was functional but lacked ambience. The only sense of a garden came from the large pear tree (*Pyrus*) in the rear and the grapevine (*Vitis*) growing on the fence to the right.

Professionals in high-pressure occupations, the owners needed a peaceful sanctuary in which they could escape their daily toils and find meaning and satisfaction in a natural but well-ordered world. This urban space, before being remade, was the exact opposite of what they needed. The place called out for harmonious arrangement. It had to be freed of its oppressive quality, separated from the surrounding world, and infused with meaning and serenity. A water garden of some sort would contribute substantially to achieving these ends.

Site design

As is so often the case, the design for this garden and its water feature arose as a response to what was already there. The site generated the desire for its opposite: hard lines would become soft curves, useless elements would be eliminated, unusable areas would be made purposeful, and each component would relate to every other through a harmony of line, color, and texture. The final effect would be a natural world contained within a strong but delicate framework.

Within this secure, masculine framework, the garden needed to be defined as a place both soothing and serene. Round and curving forms are feminine and convey a sense of softness and gentleness, which is what was called for here. A round patio would sound the keynote, and its form would influence everything surrounding it, imparting that graceful, feminine quality to everything else.

The patio, visually satisfying with its shape and size, was placed apart from the house and separated from it by plantings. This arrangement is almost always the best approach to patio placement, though it is not always easy to accomplish in a small garden. When on a patio with plants on all

BEFORE:

The garden before transformation.

A garden designed for serenity within a secure environment that comfortably contains but does not confine.

sides, you feel you are in the garden rather than on a structure that is attached to and dominated by a building. This quality is achieved by a simple stepping stone walkway that gently leads from the door, through soft plantings to both the left and right, to the patio. The patio has been set slightly apart from the walk to accentuate its round form. The path itself has

The pond, as if in response to the patio, laps its edge, then reverses around in a pleasing S curve.

STONES IN WATER, STONES OUT OF WATER

Stones that have been subjected to the influence of flowing water will be smooth and rounded, particularly if the stream or river was not recently formed. If the watercourse is fairly stable, the stones on the outside of the water flow, even if they are of the same type of rock, will be angular and rough edged. In creating the natural water garden, either rough or rounded stones can be made to work for the outside of the pond and can be effectively intermixed as well. After all, a stream that is quite active may have displaced stones from its riverbed, meaning that smooth stones are found outside the watercourse. The type or combination of stone that is used should be determined by the effect that is desired.

been given interest and intent by being built in part with large heirloom tiles bearing oriental writing meaningful to the owners. The placement, size, and shape of the patio determined the planting areas and indicated the most natural placement for the water garden.

Water feature design

The pool derives its shape in response to the patio. It traces the patio edge, repeats that curve further along its length, then reverses and curves back toward the center of the garden. This gives it an interesting shoreline, which is a pleasure for the eye to follow. It might have been tempting to create a more contemporary water feature, as the layout is somewhat contemporary; however, the natural pool harmonizes well with the garden and provides the tranquility that was desired.

Stones found in and along streams form the edging of the pool. Their primary function is to cover the water-retentive liner that must be raised above the water level and tucked into the earth beyond the pond's edge. Although round stones are not necessary on the outside of a natural pond, they carry this design's motif of rounded, curving forms to a greater level of detail. The interior of the pond is covered entirely with river rounds, and when you look into the pond, the sense that you are seeing a natural pool remains intact.

The waterfall for this pond is in keeping with the particular style of pool it feeds. It is made of the same stones as are found in and around the pond,

The interior of the pool is also stone lined, so continuing the impression of a natural pond.

with water flowing from beneath one stone and over two others that look as though they have had water flowing over them for some time. The two bottom stones are appropriately shaped in that they control the flow of the water, directing it forward and downward. Note the stones on both sides of and behind the waterfall: without these, the fall would appear unnatural. These surrounding stones anchor the waterfall and contribute to its realistic appearance. As the plants grow up behind the fall, this illusion will be further enhanced.

Planting

Again, there might have been a tendency to use very controlled planting—a boxwood hedge around the patio, for example—but again, that would have created an environment too like the controlled environments from which these homeowners sought to escape. To create the effect of structure balanced with nature, loose and airy ornamental grasses (such as *Miscanthus sinensis* 'Gracillimus') were planted alternately with red-leaf rose (*Rosa rubrifolia*) around the patio. This arrangement gives a definite sense of order while remaining delightfully free and non-restrictive. Planting beds elsewhere were given curvy lines to harmonize with the patio, as were the lawn and washed stone "beach."

The planting around the pool is of woodsy perennials, namely ferns, anemones, and ornamental grasses. To the far end of the pond behind the waterfall, a dwarf Japanese maple (*Acer palmatum*) and Hinoki cypress dominate. These plants will form a multitiered canopy over the fall, contributing considerably to the beauty and naturalness of the water garden.

An elegant environment is given structure through the organization of natural materials in organic forms that are repeated throughout the garden in, for example, a rounded patio, curved arbor, pebbled beds, and so on. It exudes an aura of tranquility from the interrelations of components, with the pool as the understated focal point of the garden. The pond's curvy lines and natural materials reflect the same qualities of peaceful tranquility, and it contributes substantially to the overall environment both visually and audibly.

A Walled Garden with Informal Fish Pool

Site condition

This site, a walled rectangle with wonderful potential, was in serious need of development. Though possessed of numerous plants, the site was not really a garden (in that it had no order to it whatsoever) and certainly not a landscape. There was no organization of space, and, except for a small area in the rear, no place for outdoor living. It was uninviting, not particularly pleasant to behold, and for the most part not usable. In short, here was a tremendous waste waiting to be reclaimed, organized, and rendered into something both attractive and usable.

Site design

A long, narrow setting such as this cannot be effectively used as a single area; it lends itself very well to division, however. The space was divided into three different "rooms," each with a different look and offering different sorts of experiences and sensory pleasures. There is the front, informal garden room, the transitional, alcove room, and the rear, formal garden. These are unified by the existing brick walls and the addition of the wrought-iron work that runs the length of the side walls and also on the end wall, where it has been built slightly higher.

An arbor leads the visitor from the front garden room to the second room, the alcove, which is designed for private use by one or two people. As the plants grow up both sides of the iron arbor, the alcove will become completely secluded, not visible from neighboring buildings or from anywhere else in the garden.

Beyond the alcove, the formal garden room is partially glimpsed and sensed but not completely. Its invisibility is due in part to the screening of the pergola and to the entrance to the pergola being set at the far right of the garden, perpendicular to the long axis of the garden. The existence of this room is clearly visible when seen from above, but from within the garden, there is the element of surprise and discovery. The formal garden possesses its own water feature, A Fountain Court, which is discussed in chapter 3. This chapter focuses on the front, informal garden.

In the new design, the front garden was to be the primary entertaining area in an informal setting. It was designed to accommodate a good-sized table,

BEFORE:

A garden that contains a confusion of plants and little usable space.

The garden space after construction had begun.

The site was designed as three, interconnected garden "rooms."

chairs, and a barbecue, and be spacious enough to hold ten or more people and a natural water garden that will provide both visual and auditory pleasure. The desired effect was for a carefree, natural charm in a lush setting that would lead naturally and gracefully to the other reaches of the garden.

Water feature design

It is important in the design of a water garden that will become so thoroughly a part of the space it occupies and be in such close proximity to the primary living areas that its placement and size not interfere with inevitable use, nor that it occupy, visually, too much or too little of the area.

The little fish pool in this garden might have been slightly larger but for the fear of encroaching too much on the usable space. Such a concession must often be made in narrow sites. Another problem associated with narrow sites is that they tend to confine the water garden to straight lines. Every opportunity to build in curves should be taken in the creation of a natural pool. Although this pool hugs the wall, it is built out from the wall in several places, which gives curves to the far edge of the pond and also varies the width of the planting beds between the far edge of the pool and the brick wall. These curves help integrate the pond with the garden it occupies. The pool is large enough to be in scale with this garden room and to provide visual and audible pleasure without being in the way of normal garden use.

The way traffic is directed around this pool also helps to integrate it into the design of the garden. The pool sweeps outward, toward the center of the garden by the arbor, creating a narrowing of paved area that visitors are instinctively drawn into, thus leading them into the next garden room, the alcove.

Notice that the far wall on this pool is elevated. Normally, in-ground water features of this style do not have such a construction. This modification was necessitated by the exposed concrete foundation of the brick wall, which would have made an inappropriate backdrop to a natural pool. River rounds were used to make the wall since they simulate a natural appearance, and even though they are mortared, they were carefully placed so that the wall would still convey the feel of a natural environment. This river-round wall also serves as a retaining wall, making planting with a layer of soil over the concrete foundation possible.

The waterfall issues from a berm of soil and rock at the far end of the pool. It flows over a single flat stone and falls several inches into the pool. The sound is sufficiently audible but not overwhelming, as it would have been with a higher fall. It makes a quiet, gurgling, splashing noise, and in this location it is easily visible from the kitchen's large, sliding-glass doors.

Although this water feature is confined to a small area, the built-in curves contribute to a sense of it being a natural feature.

MULTIPLE FUNCTIONS OF A WATER FEATURE

Every component of a landscape, including water features, exists as a physical entity within an overall design and helps to shape the spaces within that design. You can think of these physical entities as positive space and of unoccupied areas as negative space. Negative spaces are used for walking, standing, or moving, and their shapes are created and given form by the positive elements, the water garden, barbecue, benches, planting beds, and so on. This is why a water feature can't be stuck just anywhere. Wherever a water feature is placed, it will have a major impact on the arrangement of the garden and on the flow, feel, and usability of the entire environment.

Planting

The planting scheme is very informal particularly by its organization but also through the species used. (A few "formal" species such as the lily, the heavenly bamboo (*Nandina domestica*), and the rose, when placed within the plethora of informal plantings, are thoroughly transformed by association.) Coreopsis, clematis, hydrangeas, purple leaf sand cherries (*Prunus ×cistena*), and junipers are all massed into a sprawling spree with astilbes and a tree peony (*Paeonia potaninii*). Along the far edge of the pond there are ferns and hostas, liriope and bergenia plants, and one dwarf weeping hemlock (*Tsuga canadensis* 'Sargentii'). The combination has the effect of a well-composed wildness, and as the plants begin to grow together—which is the intent—this effect will be even more pronounced.

This long rectangular garden lent itself well to the creation of three garden rooms, each with its own flavor and function. The informal garden room near the house is comprised of a rambling, free-form layout with a natural pool tucked into one side where it is easily visible from the kitchen. The pool has a small waterfall that makes a pleasant gurgling sound, and it is balanced with a barbecue on the opposite side of the patio. In keeping with the informality of this room, an abundance of flowering plants with an open, loose structure are the primary planting elements—a variety of flowering shrubs,

An informal planting scheme adds to the natural charm of the garden.

WATERFALL MUSIC, WATERFALL NOISE

There is sometimes a tendency to create a large waterfall powered by a substantial pump. Large, dramatic waterfalls and the accompanying ponds they feed are generally appropriate in more remote areas of the garden away from living spaces. As wonderful as the sound of water falling onto water can be, the constant presence of a large volume of water splashing into a pool soon becomes deafening and tiring, exactly the opposite of a waterfall's intended purpose. In intimate areas intended for regular use, the sound of a waterfall is best appreciated if it is not continuously heard but recedes into the background or disappears altogether during conversation or when music is played.

perennials, and flowering vines. To raise the garden as high as possible, a wrought-iron sculpture was designed for the tops of the walls; it will soon be covered in the several species of clematis planted throughout the garden.

The water garden also serves to direct traffic through the arbor and into the second room.

A raised wall on the far side of the pool was necessary to create planting space above the concrete foundation of the brick wall.

Nature in a Suburban Backyard

Site condition

Picture the typical suburban backyard: an open rectangle with a few plants here and there is bordered on three sides by a fence and on one by the house. Between the house and the fences is lawn, and a patio is off the back door. This was the site before redesigning began.

A natural habitat in a suburban backyard.

TO CREATE A NATURAL LOOK, ALLOW A NATURAL PROCESS

Nature, and especially nature around water, is often sprawling, careless, and out of control. To create this look around a man-made pond, keep your pruners where they're hard to find and lose your shears altogether. Let the plants (which, if properly selected, will respond appropriately) do what they do—grow, sprawl, creep, and climb all over everything and each other. They will establish their own equilibrium, each staking out their own territory with very little assistance. In time they will take on the look of a completely natural creation.

Site design

Now picture this: A luxuriant lawn sweeps down to a lushly planted pond that is comfortably tucked into the far corner of the property, replete with fish, frogs, tadpoles, water plants, and a waterfall. Birds and squirrels and rabbits and other wildlife come here to nest and forage and play and drink and bath and just enjoy themselves. Bordering this haven of nature is a bog garden (see chapter 7) that not only supports a variety of unusual perennials and shrubs but also feeds the garden. Almost any suburban backyard could host such a lovely scene, and more should. Once established, they are easy to care for and provide a rich tapestry of nature in harmony.

Which of these two vignettes would you prefer?

Water feature design

The natural wood fence that borders the property with a variety of trees, shrubs, and vines in front of it create a pleasing and naturalistic backdrop to the pond and its plantings. The pond is irregular in shape and planted in such a way as to mask its actual borders in many places, thus increasing the impression that it is a body of water that someone edged in stone here and there. The water flowing into the pond runs down from a little rivulet that emerges from some unseen source in the undergrowth beyond. There is no way to know that this pond is not nature-made.

The depth of the pond varies but is deep enough in places to permit fish to overwinter, thus eliminating the problem of mosquitoes. This variable depth also makes possible a great range of aquatic plants, from those that need to be covered by several inches or more of water to margin plants.

Planting

The *Cedrus atlantica* in the back and the Japanese maple in the foreground, which are normally used as specimen plants and are associated with more formal settings, take on an altogether different look in this setting. Mixed as they are with the hibiscus, hostas, irises, and ferns, they appear to us as natural plant forms, distinctive but completely at home in this wild setting.

A natural pond can make a wonderful complement to a suburban backyard, transforming the ordinary into a delightful habitat for wildlife and exotic plantings. By heavily planting the background and borders of the pond and stream, you not only make the water garden seem completely natural but you also provide nesting places for wildlife.

Siting the "natural" pool

If you have a choice of where to place the pool, several factors should be considered apart from the specific aesthetic concerns I address in the project discussions. These factors regarding placement apply to any in-ground pool. A slight slope is good, particularly if you are going to have a fairly dramatic waterfall. The water flow should appear to have a reason for its direction, and a slope provides that reason. You can leave the ground sloped—or even enhance the slope where you intend to put the waterfall—while easily leveling the pond area. The pool itself should be placed on a low, level area, where it would naturally occur.

If possible, avoid placing the pond beneath trees, as such a placement will necessitate more frequent cleaning of the pond and also limit which plants you can grow in the pool because of the shade that will be generated. If there are trees everywhere, don't let this stop you, however. More frequent cleaning does not need to be a real hardship, and low-light water plants are readily available.

Do not place the pond where it will receive runoff that contains any toxic or potentially toxic chemicals as might issue from a rooftop, for example. You will probably want to have plants and fish in the pond, both of which are sensitive to foreign chemicals in the water. Even runoff that passes over cement can be toxic in effect. Cement contains lime, which raises the pH, and although fish can endure a wide range of pH levels, they do not respond well to fluctuating levels.

A final consideration in deciding where to place the pool is the effect desired, which in turn will be a function of how and when it is seen. A pond visible from a prominent room in the home can add considerably to the enjoyment of the home. Entryway ponds can be quite dramatic, yet there is also something to be said for the pond you happen across while wandering through the garden, the pond that is placed for private contemplation, or the pond that is used as an aesthetic component of a small private area.

Choosing the material for the natural pool

Several materials are available for small pond construction: reinforced concrete, rigid plastic or fiberglass liners, and flexible liners. The flexible liner is the only truly viable alternative for over 90 percent of home applications.

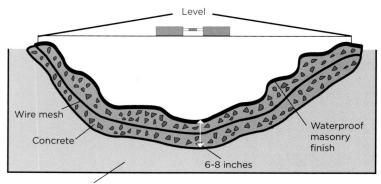

An informal concrete pool

Given the available alternatives, concrete is much too expensive and labor intensive. The rigid plastic liners tend to crack, and both the plastic and fiberglass liners are too limiting in terms of depth, shape, and size, and although I discuss rigid liners and concrete pools in detail, I will concentrate on flexible liners.

The concrete pool

The work involved in constructing a concrete pond, both in terms of complexity and sheer labor, does not even come close to what goes into building the other types of pools. A pool five feet long, three feet wide, and two feet deep will require twenty-one cubic feet of concrete, which is very difficult to mix. Nevertheless, there are those who want something really durable, and concrete is that. Plumbing and drain lines can be built into the concrete pool, but this is work for a professional and not recommended for the average pond builder. The concrete pool I describe how to build has no built-in plumbing.

Concrete pool installation

YOU WILL NEED: *waterproof cement, sand gravel, marble dust, shovel, trowel, float, wheelbarrow, mason's line, line level, carpenter's level, two-by-four, mixing pan, and wire mesh.*

Excavate for a pool, allowing about twelve inches extra all around it to make up for the concrete shell and the stone that will go over the shell. Thus, if you want your pond to be six feet by four feet by three feet, then excavate a site that is eight feet by six feet by four feet. (Add one foot to each end and each side, and one foot to the bottom.) There is no need to build in much detail at this point as you can create shelving and other such features in the concrete itself; just try to get the general contour as you would like it to be in the end.

With this amount of concrete (about twenty-one cubic feet), it is probably worthwhile renting a small gas- or electric-powered mixer as mixing concrete by hand is a very difficult job. Make your concrete mix about two parts Portland cement, two parts gravel, and four to six parts sand. Cut and lay in your wire mesh everywhere there is to be concrete. The wire provides a unifying framework for the concrete and helps prevent cracking. The thickness of the wire mesh will depend on how cold it gets in your area. If you experience consistently freezing temperatures, use as heavy a grade as you can work with. For more temperate regions, chicken wire will suffice.

Shovel the cement in, making sure it is at least eight inches thick where the pool's sides meet its bottom and at least six inches thick everywhere else. Trowel it smooth but do not overwork the cement. If you have to stop the job and continue it the next day, deeply scar and rough all the edges that will be binding to the next day's batch of cement. Before applying the new cement to the old, apply an agent (I use Weldcrete) that will bind green (freshly hardened) to wet cement. Keep the work covered with plastic after each day's work and let it dry covered. After the cement is hard, it should be filled with water and left to sit a few days as this makes a harder shell.

After a few days, drain the shell and mix up a batch of marble dust (which is used instead of sand) and cement following the directions on the bag of marble dust. This mix is the watertight, plaster coating that will be troweled on in two or three coats over the concrete shell. Keep this sealed shell moist too by covering it until it is hard. Alternatively, there is a material called Wet-seal, a product that makes wet areas waterproof, not just water resistant, which has given me good results. It is mixed as a slurry and, like the marble dust, is painted on the concrete surface. When this marble dust plaster or Wet-seal is dry, the shell is ready to hold water. Fill it and let it sit for several days to be sure it does. Mark the water line, cover the water to lessen evaporation, then check the water line after a day. If the water line remains steady, construction can continue, but if it has dropped significantly, allow the water to remain without refilling. If the water level drops to a given level and remains there, check along that line for visible cracks. If you find a crack, replaster this area and refill the shell with water. If you do not find a crack, replaster the entire shell. It is unlikely you will have to repeat these steps, however, if you have followed these directions.

Once you have built the shell, you have completed the major portion of the labor. The rest of the work involves aesthetics. You can build in-stone planters using cement or a house for the pump or you can mortar stone to the bottom and sides of the pool to make it look as natural as possible. Be sure to follow the directions for hiding the pump, pump electric line, and hose as described in Stoning the Pond later in this chapter and in the waterfall construction sections.

The excavation, leveled on all sides and ready for the flexible liner that will be placed in this natural pool.

The rigid liner pool

The rigid liner offers the least flexibility in terms of shape, size, and depth while offering the greatest ease of installation. If this is the type you decide to use, and if you intend to lay stones in the interior to simulate a natural pond, choose one that is larger than the body of water you want.

Rigid or preformed liner installation

YOU WILL NEED: *marking material (such as chalk, garden lime, or marking paint), shovel, mason's line and line level, and carpenter's level.*

Flip the pool upside down where you want it to be and outline the top edge with chalk, lime, or marking paint. Flip it back and keep it to the side. Measure about two inches out from the line you've marked to allow for the sand that you will place inside and begin excavation. Try to reproduce the slant of the liner walls.

Next measure inside the liner to determine how deep the shelf is. Also measure the width of the shelf at various points around the liner. Transfer these measurements to the excavation and dig out an area for the shelf, adding two inches for sand. Measure the liner again to obtain the shape and total depth of the bottom of the pool and excavate for this, again adding two inches. The hole you dig should roughly match the liner.

Check for level all across the top of the excavation with the line and line level and check the level of the bottom and the shelves with the carpenter's level. Make any adjustments and remove any rocks or roots from the excavation. Drop the liner in and see how it fits. It should be about two inches below grade and must be perfectly level across all sides. Again, make adjustments as necessary. Remove the liner, add two inches of sand to the bottom of the excavation and to the shelf, and place the liner in. Move it around to settle it into place. Check for level. When everything is level, go all around the sides and pour sand between the liner and the excavation anywhere there is space. Begin filling the liner with water and occasionally water in the sand along the sides as you go. Refill any holes between the liner and the excavation with sand. Pump out the dirty water from the liner, place the planted pots in the liner, and refill. Wait several days before adding fish and then add them slowly, one or two at a time, with several days between additions, as water pH must stabilize before fish will survive. If you want the pond to look more natural, you will need to add stones, which I describe in detail later in this chapter.

Flexible liners

The two kinds of flexible liners most in use are the butyl rubber pond liner, a synthetic rubber made from rubber polymers, and the ethylene propylene diene monomer (EPDM) liner. The primary differences between these two are in flexibility and cost, the butyl liner being the most flexible and the most expensive. Both types are durable under water and soil, and both are puncture resistant, though the thicker EPDM will take more mechanical abuse. The butyl liner comes in a variety of thicknesses, usually of thirty or forty mil. (Mil is a measurement of thickness equivalent to 0.025 millimeters or 0.001 inches.) Some suppliers recommend thirty mil for small ponds because of the flexibility and ease of eliminating folds. However, if stones are used throughout the pond to cover the surface, folds don't matter. The EPDM is widely available in forty mil and can sometimes be found in sixty-mil thicknesses.

Flexible liner installation

YOU WILL NEED: *liner, underliner, shovel, carpenter's level, mason's line, line level, and marking material (such as chalk, garden lime, or marking paint).*

The excavation with shelving for a two-tiered water garden.

Once the site has been determined, the pool must be designed on the ground. Many people use a garden hose to lay out the pool's shape but powdered chalk, bagged lime, or marking paint, available at many building supply and hardware stores, work well too. When drawing the intended pool on the ground, remember to make it about a foot wider and longer (and a little deeper) than the body of water you wish to see, as the materials will take up space. Also exaggerate the curves. They tend to flatten out in construction.

The hole you excavate should have shelves built into it at different levels. They can hold plants in pots, should you decide to use pots, and the stone, which will help improve the aesthetics of the pond. By creating shelves within the water garden, you shorten its vertical planes, which makes the sides of the pool easier to cover in stone. If you were to make the pool with no shelves, its sides would be as tall as the pool is deep, and covering them with stone is problematic.

Most authorities recommend you begin excavating the pond from the deepest part and work outward. Another approach is to begin excavating the outside line to about half a foot, then to continue excavating from the center outward, alternating between the two until the excavations meet. Make the shelves as level as possible or pitch them upward slightly so that the outer

HALF NATURAL IS UNNATURAL

When attempting to create the illusion of a "natural" water feature, you must take into consideration every visible component. A pond with a natural shape that is edged in natural stone will not look natural if it has a visible rubber interior or pump.

edge of the shelves is higher than the inner edge. Make sure the shelves are wide enough—at least eight inches—to take pots and stones. This kind of shelf makes it less likely that plants in pots will fall over. Make the vertical sides of the shelves as short as possible so the liner is easily hidden by fewer and smaller stones. The depth of the pool should be such that the water does not freeze to the bottom. If given six inches to a foot of water, fish will survive beneath the ice and require no feeding during winter months.

Instead of placing potted plants on shelves you can create depressions in the soil during excavation and then add cat litter or sand mixed with soil to those depressions once the liner is in place. These holes are then planted and covered with small river stones before the pool is filled with water and after construction is done. The plants tend to grow over and cover the liner.

Among the easier mistakes to make in digging the pond is to fail to provide adequate space for the pump. The size of the space needed is a function of the pump and filtration system, as well as where in the pond the pump is to go. Three factors should be considered: water recirculation—it is best to have the pump on the opposite side of the pond from the waterfall or return line to provide maximum circulation and aeration of the water; visibility—neither the pump nor its electric cord or return hose should be seen; and accessibility—the pump should be easily removed. This means that wherever you place the pump (on a shelf or in a depression created to hold the pump), be sure to wrap sufficient electric cord and waterline around it so the pump and filter can be completely and easily removed for rinsing. Before determining what size and style of pump and filter to use, read the section on filtration systems.

When you've finished the excavation, check elevations with a level set on top of a two-by-four or with a string line level to make sure all the edges of the pond are level with one another. A low point will determine the water level, and anything above that point will appear as raised wall, which is usually unsightly. If there is a low point, you can either add soil to that edge or lower the other edges. Remove any stones or large roots from the excavation and you are ready to line the excavation.

Lining the pond

To determine the size of the liner to use, measure the length of the bottom and the height of the two end walls and add two feet. Do the same for the width of the excavation. If, for example, you determine that you need a twelve-foot by fifteen-foot liner, including the two extra feet you added to each dimension, then that would be what most sources would tell you to order. Experience has taught me, however, that if I need a twelve by fifteen feet liner, it is best to purchase a fifteen by twenty liner. This lesson is a result of having decided in the eleventh hour to change the shape or increase the depth of the pond. It can be intensely frustrating to find you're one inch shy of enough material to complete the pool as you'd like it, and although you can bind one liner to another liner, it is not an easy or convenient thing to do, especially once the liner is in place. Put simply, it is better to pay a few dollars more than to risk having too small a liner. When determining the size of the liner, you'll also want to allow extra material for the area around the waterfall for reasons I explain later.

Before placing the liner in the ground, it is generally wise to use an underliner. This is a feltlike material that is effective in preventing punctures from things such as small stones. It is inexpensive, can be purchased in square-feet sheets or by the roll from the same sources that sell liners, and is useful under stones on top of the liner. To lay in the underliner, cut a piece to the right size, lay it over the excavation, and drop it in.

An aside here: it is much easier to build a pond with four hands than with two. With a helper, you can, for example, position the underliner or liner over the pond and drop them right in. Alone, you will have to drag each of them over, often knocking debris into the excavation and breaking your neatly excavated walls. Ponds can be built alone, but it is better with help.

With one person in the pond at its center and the other on the outside, begin working all the way around the pool in one direction, getting the underliner to lie as flat as possible against all surfaces, folding it into pleats where it appears natural to do so. When the underliner is as flat as possible, drop in the liner. Then carefully get into the pond (you might want to do this in your socks or with felt tied around your boots) and fold the liner into pleats as you did the underliner. Try not to step on the edges of the shelves as they break easily, making later pot placement difficult or impossible. Be sure you have sufficient liner material all around the outside edges of your excavation with two feet or more where you plan to have the waterfall.

As you fill the hole with water, the liner is pulled into the hole, filling any voids. If some sides are shorter than others, place stones along these shorter edges so that the liner will be pulled into the hole from the other sides where it's longer. Once the pond is filled, it is best to let it sit for at least an hour or even overnight to be absolutely certain there are no leaks. Mark the water level before you leave, then note if there is any decline. Once you are convinced the integrity of the liner has not been compromised, you can begin the real work—making the water garden look good—and for this you will want to drain the pond. But a word of caution first: At this point you see where the edges of your pond are going to be and there is a real temptation to cut off the excess liner. Don't. Many a pond builder has been absolutely certain where the pond should end and has cut away the liner, only to later

A newly filled pond with the underliner and liner still showing. Note the stones inside the pond.

Beginning to stone the pond.

regret it. Let removing what you know beyond all doubt is excess liner be the last thing you do—and even then don't do it. Bury it instead, as you may need it in the future.

Stoning the pond

The following instructions are for placing stones in any natural pond. Once the flexible or rigid liner or concrete pool is in place, the aesthetic work of placing river stone begins. A pool will rarely look absolutely natural but any pond can look quite good if the right stones are used and if some sensitivity is employed in their placement. The stones in the pond should be water worn (they are referred to as river rock, river flats, or river rounds). The stones outside the pond do not need to be water worn but should not be too dissimilar from the river rocks. Use larger stones against the vertical surfaces and smaller stone and river pebbles on the horizontal surfaces. Try not to stack them, but do place the larger rocks on the bottom so they naturally support the smaller stones above. Rocks of varying sizes, in combination with the water and margin plants, will help create a natural, pleasing look.

Cover all unnatural elements, such as the pump and filter, electrical cords, and waterlines with the stones. Be sure, however, that you have left enough hose and electric line in a cavity with the pump and filter. I recommend doing this because if the pump or filter needs to be lifted from its location in the pond (say by three feet) for cleaning, then three feet of cord and hose must be kept coiled with the pump and not covered with stones.

If you don't want to see plastic or clay pots in your pond, build planters with the river stones and cement them together in pleasing shapes. Planters built this way will blend into the pond bottom and sides. If you build them at different elevations they will provide excellent, permanent planting places for all your aquatics. Once the inside of the pond has been stoned, you can make the outside of the pond look good with stone too, but try to avoid making a necklace of stones around the perimeter of the pond. If at all possible, extend the stonework to surrounding areas and build in planting pockets. You are next ready to build the waterfall (see chapter 6).

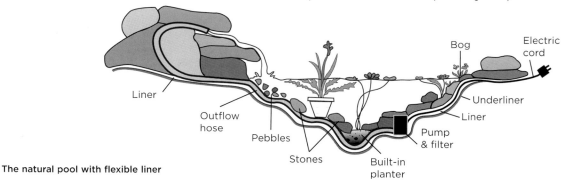

The natural pool with flexible liner

2

Raised, Informal Pools

A Natural Haven

Site condition

This was a fairly dismal site, cramped, barren, darkly shadowed by an overhanging ailanthus tree, and charmless. Putting a water garden here without completely transforming the site would only have made the place more dank and less inviting. Yet how could this transformation take place? One excellent way to approach such a problem is to ask: What do I want to see here? How would I use the space?

Site design

As it happened, the owners wanted the garden to serve as a personal sanctuary, one that could also be used to entertain small groups. They wanted the garden to be attractive from the overlooking deck as well as pleasurable to inhabit, and they wanted it in a natural, organic style.

To begin to achieve all this, planting areas first had to be created. Since roots from the ailanthus tree were everywhere, raised beds had to be built to provide a viable planting space for the many shrubs and perennials that would help create a natural setting. In keeping with the desire for an organic quality to predominate, a natural stone was chosen for the walls of the raised beds. The walls were built without mortar and were laid on a graceful curve. The raised beds made it possible to create boundaries of foliage and blossom, masking the hard lines of the property with beautiful plants. They also brought graceful motion to the space through the natural medium of stone, thus providing the perfect setting for a natural, raised water garden.

Water feature design

The water garden was designed to be an integral component, not only of the entire setting but also of the raised plane to which it belongs. In such a location, the water garden takes up the least amount of living space and provides the maximum impact from all parts of the garden and from the overlooking deck. It "belongs" in this setting and provides a pleasant, textural contrast to the stone and foliage. Placed on the angle, the water feature does not force itself upon or dominate the garden but rather offers itself as an interrelated element within the entire landscape, so adding richness and variety.

BEFORE:

An unpromising site seemed too dismal to host a water feature.

The garden space transformed,
complete with a raised, natural pool.

The rear wall from which the water flows into the pond is raised slightly above the outer wall, which creates a nice tiered effect. Behind this back wall are plants that, in time, will arch over it, adding another dimension and also softening the stonework. Both the rear and retaining walls were built of the same kind of stone, but smooth river stones were placed in the rear wall where the water flows. Though this water garden is not intended to make one believe it is naturally occurring, it is intended to feel natural and organic, which it does through the materials used and the manner in which it is built.

The original garden design called for only the first pool (the one on the left), but the owner later requested that the pond be extended to the right. Between the two adjoining pools, a stone bridge was built beneath which water flows and fish swim. The first pool was probably more in scale with the tiny garden, but the additional pool works too and it allows for more fish and water plants.

Planting

This garden offers several lessons in planting schemes for small spaces. The outstanding impression the garden makes is one of astonishing lushness in a natural setting. There is a wealth of textures, a variety of foliar colors in countless shades, and many different plant forms, all providing richness and diversity. Yet this garden does not feel "busy" or eclectic. Why is that? The answer lies in the unity that has been created through the repetition not only of plants with the same leaf and plant forms but also of plant combinations that have the same or similar plant and leaf qualities. For example, the bold leaf and broad form of *Hydrangea macrophylla* 'Mariesii' contrasts superbly with the variegated iris, while their variegations also harmonize with each other. This theme of combinations displaying both harmony and contrast is carried through on a smaller scale in the combination of the variegated dwarf berberis and variegated liriope plants and, on an even smaller scale, in the variegated leaves of the euonymus and thyme plants.

These groupings transition into the dark, glossy-leaved holly (*Ilex*), creating a vivid foliar contrast, while a red osier dogwood (*Cornus sericea*) picks up the variegation theme and deepens the contrast because of its proximity to the *Ilex cornuta*. Below that grouping, the dark, glossy-leaved *Gaultheria procumbens* echoes the holly while also contrasting with the variegated liriope. Throughout the garden the grassy leaves of irises and ornamental grasses such as *Pennisetum* contrast with the bold-leaved plants, and the sedums that here and there spill over the wall, together with the many vines

The water garden is not symmetrically placed, so does not dominate the garden, as suits a natural design.

(clematis hybrids in this case), all work to bind the garden. All these plants provide a rich tapestry while uniting the garden into a diverse yet singular place. There is no end of detail to attract and please the eye, yet the garden possesses a quality of peacefulness the owners so wanted.

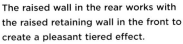

The raised wall in the rear works with the raised retaining wall in the front to create a pleasant tiered effect.

This garden needed to be elevated above the ravenous roots of the ailanthus tree, a necessity that, coupled with the owners' wish for a natural, organic garden, gave rise to the design scheme. A curving stone wall built without mortar created the planting beds and provided the perfect setting for the water garden.

Water issues from the rear, raised wall and tumbles over a series of smooth river rocks into the pool below. The water garden is retained by the front wall, which is aesthetically pleasing in itself, and it offers a place to sit and watch the fish or tend the water plants. The overall design is unified by the stone of the walls, the water garden, and a rich but carefully chosen planting scheme.

Water emerges from the rear wall and splashes over smooth stones into the pool below. Fish swim beneath the bridge between the two portions of the pool.

Raised Pools in a Public Space

BEFORE 1:

The author preparing the site for construction.

BEFORE 2:

Foundations for the walls being excavated.

Site condition

This conservatory of music in Brooklyn, New York, was undergoing a complete reconstruction and the site was an open canvas on which anything was possible—within certain parameters, that is. The garden needed to allow private contemplation while accommodating groups of various sizes, and it needed to handle considerable traffic, including many children. The entrance to the conservatory was being moved from a busy avenue to a quiet side street, so the garden entrance had to attract visitors in a pleasant, welcoming way and lead them gracefully to the building entrance. Finally, as the garden was a part of a school of music, it should also be lyrical and harmonious.

Site design

Too often institutions are dominated by functionality with too little regard for aesthetics and simple pleasures. Entryways usually lead directly to the front door in a rigid, linear way without providing agreeable experiences along the way. Here was not just the opportunity but the mandate to create something a bit more responsive to human sensibilities and aesthetic appreciation. This garden entry would have to set the appropriate tone for studying and listening to music by establishing the right atmosphere upon entry into the conservatory and then maintaining the appropriate mood upon departure.

Water, and particularly water in motion, is a thoroughly appropriate element for a musical motif. A stream running through the garden and connecting two raised, informal pools offers a range of visual, audio, and visceral pleasures, all of which are an apt metaphor for the purpose of this institution—music. Likewise, the curving walkway metaphor breaks out of the usual institutional pattern and gently guides visitors through a garden setting before leading them to the conservatory's main entrance.

Several seating areas along the way to the conservatory's entrance invite the visitor to rest within the tranquil environment, and various details, such as the tiles with a musical motif that are built into the brick walls, add textural and tonal qualities. These attributes combine to give the visitor a complete—and completely enjoyable—environment suitable for studying and listening to music, for contemplation, and for engaging in group activities

AFTER 1: Water flows from a raised, informal fountain and along a stream to an informal fountain below.

AFTER 2: Breaking out of the paradigm typical of institutions, the garden leads the visitor along a meandering path and past a nearby stream.

FIRST IMPRESSIONS LAST

Whenever possible, it is far better to direct an entry walk away from the building and through a garden area and to give it a pleasing line. We tend to say that we want a direct, straight walk to the door and that we will only cut through to the most direct route anyway, but this is not so. Once a curving or indirect walk is in place, we do use it, and if the route is made pleasant, we also appreciate it. The entrance to a home or any other building is usually the first impression the place makes on us. It is the last impression we have on leaving; often it is also a lasting one. When making a garden, resist functionality and encourage aesthetics.

in an informal yet sophisticated setting. They also make coming and going a pleasure.

Water feature design

Before renovation, the primary entrance was on the main avenue, where it was easily noticed. The new entrance was around the corner on a side street and it tended to be overlooked. To draw attention to the entry, I designed a slightly oversized, raised fountain immediately inside the gates several feet from the sidewalk. This fountain would sound the keynote, announcing the garden entrance to people looking for the school and to those just passing by.

The upper pool needed to balance and harmonize with the brick and brownstone walls adjacent to and across from it, but, as it is also the source of the stream, it needed to take on a naturalistic style. The pool, therefore, begins on the left as a brick and brownstone construction and then transitions gradually into a river-stone creation. The river stone continues through the rest of the water garden and into its interior of the pool as well. This same transitioning composition was required in the lower pool because it serves as both a water garden and a continuation of the walls.

The upper water garden consists of two pools, the smaller one spilling into the larger. The purpose was to create sound and motion that would attract attention in a pleasing but subtle way. The lower pool spills over a waterfall and into the stream that flows down to the bottom water garden. (I discuss the stream in detail in the section on streams in chapter 6.)

The lower water garden also consists of two pools. The stream flows into

One of the seating areas overlooking the upper pool.

the upper, in-ground pool that spills over a weir and into the lower pool. The purpose here was not so much the achievement of a certain appearance and sound but rather the creation of motion in the lower body of water. As the terminus of the entire system, the water could become too still in the further extremities of the pool if not for the water flowing over the weir.

Clearly, the pools in this garden are not "natural" pools, and nor are they formal. They are asymmetrical in shape, are above ground, and built of irregularly shaped and sized river rocks, which is what prevents them from being formal. Though they are not natural pools, considerable care was taken in selecting the river rocks to help convey a naturalistic feel to them.

In addition to being an attractive feature of the landscape, this water garden serves as a part of the wall and helps to direct traffic flow. While the upper pool defines the entrance to the garden and directs the flow of traffic down toward the building entrance, the lower pool, with its counterpoint wall across the walk, guides visitors directly into the building while accenting and defining the pathway out of the property.

Both pools are meant to be enjoyed as visitors enter and leave the garden and from seating areas within the garden. The upper seating area with its two benches commands a refreshing view over the water of the upper pool, and a small seating area lies just before the lower pool. Planting pockets in each pool were created from stone to eliminate or reduce the need for pots. Together these pools provide altogether different, exciting, and agreeable experiences—altogether different from what is found in most institution entrances. They become reasons in themselves for visiting this conservatory.

This portion of the garden is planted in soft pastels in the blue and pink range for romantic effect.

Images of Claude Debussy and many other composers, artists, and musical instruments adorn the walls of the garden walk.

Slightly oversized, the raised, upper pool attracts visitors and draws them into the garden.

The upper pool is also a wall designed to harmonize with the walls across from and adjacent to it. In addition, the wall was designed to transform gradually into a naturalistic water garden.

A natural, in-ground pool flowing into a raised, informal pool.

Planting

The garden is planted for a romantic feel with flower color in the blue and pink scheme. These colors are suitable for the theme of the garden and they harmonize and contrast well with the brick of the building and walls. There are azaleas, camellias, hydrangeas, crape myrtles (*Lagerstroemia indica*), *Anemone* species, plants of *Caryopteris*, and three cultivars of flowering cherries, namely *Prunus serrulata* 'Kwanzan', *P. serrulata* 'Royal Burgundy', and *P. subhirtella* 'Pendula'. Ornamental grasses such as miscanthus and pennisetum, a variety of creeping ground covers, and a few annuals and bulbs randomly planted round out the planting beds.

Nearer the building, strong groupings of deciduous and evergreen shrubs predominate. There we find *Ilex aquifolium* 'Silver Edge', *Cornus sericea*, *Pieris japonica*, *Cercis canadensis* 'Forest Pansy', and *Hydrangea paniculata* 'Tardiva'. *Heucherella* 'Rosalie' is at the front.

This garden needed to satisfy a variety of requirements, both practical and aesthetic. As the primary entrance to the Brooklyn Conservatory of Music, it needed to control the flow of traffic to and from the entry door, accommodate gatherings of people, and provide quiet recesses for private study. As a symbol of this institution's purpose, it was important for the entry garden to be gracefully lyrical and offer a wealth of sensory enjoyments within a texturally rich, harmonious composition. It was intended that the garden exhibit a strong and enduring framework containing elements of delicacy and transience. Water was used extensively, in part because it possesses these latter qualities, in part because of the natural and historical associations between water and music, and in part because water on display is such an inviting and satisfying element.

RELATING MATERIALS TO FUNCTION

It is perfectly fine—and often desirable—to combine different kinds of materials within the same setting and even within the same structure. Such a combination often provides enjoyable textural and color contrasts and harmonies. It is important, however, that the materials used for a given structure relate well to both the function and the style of that structure. Just as a waterfall is built in a natural style using real boulders would not succeed (unless very particular care is taken to accomplish the integration) if it flowed into a rectangular tile basin, neither would a rectangular brick fountain flowing into a natural stream be convincing. The fountain and the waterfall would have different, opposing effects upon the viewer, the one canceling out the other. When working within a given style, it is necessary, as a rule, to employ materials that reflect that style. When a structure must perform more than one distinct function (such as a wall transitioning into a raised pool), different materials can be incorporated and blended together.

Deciduous and broadleaf evergreens create rich foliar contrasts and harmonies.

A Raised Pool in a Children's Garden

BEFORE:

A small property made still smaller through poor division.

After opening the site and eliminating whatever was unessential, the true measure of the space became apparent.

Site condition

Initially, this small yard violated nearly every principle of gracious design. A few overgrown plants took up a lot of space with many encroaching neighboring plants. The space was linear, cluttered, uninteresting, and poorly divided into three unusable planes. The result was an area that seemed much smaller than it really was.

Site design

In addition to finding a design appropriate to the site itself that would be gracious and attractive, I needed to address all the family's particular requirements for the garden. The family wanted the space to be fun and interesting as well as beautiful and serviceable. They hoped to use the garden in every way possible, including for entertaining, cooking, and dining, and the children needed plenty of room to play. The space is only nineteen feet wide by twenty-two feet deep; clearly, usable space would need to be created as the site was transformed into a true garden. As is often the case, more space was available here than was at first apparent.

The space was too small to accommodate more than two distinct areas, but one large living area bordered on three sides with raised beds would work well. Raised areas would allow for abundant plantings not subject to the vigor of children's feet, and the larger, paved area would provide ample outdoor living space. Tiles of various animals and of the family members' names were randomly built into the wall, so contributing to the qualities of lightness and fun. In keeping with a free-form design, curvy walls that wind in and out and rise and fall with gentle curves delineate the beds. To remain true to the Victorian-style house, the walls were made of used brick.

Water feature design

A raised fountain was a natural outcome of the raised beds winding through the garden. It was the perfect element to serve as the anchor to the walls and as a focal point within an asymmetrical layout. A raised fountain also represented a practical decision, as an in-ground pool would too easily become, through the inspiration of children, a swimming hole, however inadvertently.

Placed centrally along the long axis, the raised fountain functions as a major focal point from everywhere within the garden. However, because of its shape, it contributes to the informal layout. The fountain's placement also creates private space behind it, which the owner requested, a place where he could sit and peacefully read beneath the weeping cherry (*Prunus subhirtella* 'Pendula') while enjoying the fountain.

Used brick was chosen for the water fountain and the walls as it has a warmer, more comfortable feel than does new brick, and both the interior and exterior of the fountain are ornamented with tiles of water animals.

Planting

I chose plants of an informal character in keeping with the overall theme and that provided a range of sensory experiences throughout the seasons. The only existing plant that remained in the garden was the river birch (*Betula nigra*). However, the neighboring larch (*Larix kaempferi*) and the false cypress to the rear lend their beauty to the garden. To these were added fruit-bearing blueberry plants (*Vaccinium corymbosum*), from which breakfast can be picked, and plants that emit a pleasant fragrance when brushed, such as lavender (*Lavandula*), which were placed near the wall where the children like to walk and by their stone-seat in the garden near the butterfly house.

Grasses such as *Pennisetum* remain attractive through the winter, as do the oak-leaf hydrangea and the berry-bearing plants of holly and *Skimmia*. A honeysuckle (*Lonicera* ×*heckrottii*) lends its sweet perfumes and, together with roses and clematis, covers the lattice. Numerous flowering perennials such as coreopsis and anemone brighten the garden from early spring to early winter. Hydrangeas are well represented with *Hydrangea macrophylla*, *H. paniculata*, and *H. quercifolia*, and beneath the weeping cherry is a mixture of rhododendron hybrids, *Cornus alba* 'Elegantissima', and various ferns.

Overall, the planting is light, leafy, and seemingly arbitrary, yet it is unified by a repetition of species, textural qualities, and foliage color. Irises, liriopes, and the various grasses, for example, provide vertical accents throughout the garden, while the variegations in the *Cornus sericea*, the liriopes, and some of the irises help tie it all together.

The planting is intentionally dense with every planting space used to the maximum effect. In some of the marginal areas along the fence on the right, for example, where it is difficult to grow anything, *Houttuynia cordata* clambers at the foot of the Japanese cedar, which stands as sentry to the private seating area and makes a rich backdrop to the climbing rose. Nearby *Pieris japonica* provides a handsome accent while a *Leucothoë* specimen brings an informal element to the congregation. Although this style of planting

Tiles of animals and of the family members' names decorate the walls.

NEVER UNDERESTIMATE THE NEGATIVE INFLUENCE OF BAD DESIGN

Many small sites seem so much smaller and more restrictive than they are simply because of what has or has not been done to them. To really understand a site's potential, it is necessary to imagine it without all the elements that can and should be eliminated. Inappropriate terracing, badly placed planting or walking areas, misplaced walls, unfortunate location of dominant trees, overhanging foliage from neighboring sites—simply eliminating these will begin to expose the hidden potential of the site.

The completed garden with raised fountain.

requires regular, light pruning to keep one plant from dominating another, it makes for the most beautiful as well as the most enjoyable kind of space to garden and in which to be.

First and most importantly, the space was designed to create a sense of unity with each of the components contributing to the overall effect. A quality environment, it was meant to be strong and durable yet also light, airy, charming, and whimsical. The undulant brick walls contribute very much to this effect of both lightness and strength. A two-course brick wall is a serious or formal element but this one winds in and out and rises and falls, its uneven height and undulating motion all adding to the sense of whimsy. It is also decorated with animals in relief, contains built-in benches, and terminates in a curvy water garden, where water spews from the mouth of a fairly bizarre frog. The winding stairs and arching arbor, together with the undulant walls and water garden, all work to produce an environment that is functional yet also fun and graceful. River flats and river pebbles were built into the paving to create some light relief on that plane, and the abundant, seemingly carefree planting completes the picture.

DIFFERENCES BETWEEN GARDENS AND COLLECTIONS OF PLANTS

Plants people generally concern themselves with making sure every plant has enough space in which to reach its maximum size. Although such an approach gives rise to beautiful specimens, it is arguable as to whether it gives rise to a beautiful garden. From this author's perspective, the most enjoyable and beautiful gardens are those in which plants grow together in forming a richly diverse unity of foliage and flower. These gardens require regular but very light pruning. When the hydrangea, for example, begins to overcome the skimmia, a branch or portion of the hydrangea can be removed. It still looks beautiful, as does the skimmia beneath it, and both go on living well together in a beautiful, harmonious unity.

Plants of *Cryptomeria*, *Houttuynia*, *Leucothoë*, and *Pieris*, together with a rose, make a rich textural and floral combination.

A curved brick wall with hand-carved tiles forms a raised bed that is also functional.

A Symphony in Brick

Site condition

A plane of concrete bordered by walls and fences created a space dominated by horizontal and vertical rectangles, a space that was thoroughly uninviting. The area made a good basketball court, perhaps, but was certainly not something that could be called a garden. Removing the existing concrete would prove too expensive, and, being an urban environment, this property would of course have to retain the fence and walls between it and the adjoining property.

Site design

Although concrete could have been removed from specified areas and planting beds built in their place, that would not have been sufficient to overcome the static quality of the hard, rectangular planes. Instead, raised planters with flowing curves were designed for both sides of the property. These planters bring a tremendous sense of motion and, through the counterpoint created by their offset placement, rhythm. This sense, even more than the plants, serves to mitigate the hard rigidity of the site. And although the owner wanted an environment that was pleasingly graceful, she also wanted structure. Brick laid in these curving forms gave her both.

Water feature design

The raised pool arose naturally out of the overall design; it could just as easily have been another planter, mirroring its counterpart from across the garden. As a water garden, however, it brings other textural dimensions—motion, sound, and water-life—while contributing to the overall effect of smooth-flowing motion within a strong structure.

Planting

Above the water garden arches a *Deutzia gracilis* 'Magician', and behind that is a leyland cypress (×*Cupressocyparis leylandii*). Below the cypress, a spreading juniper (*Juniperus horizontalis*), a tree peony (*Paeonia suffruticosa*), and several azaleas fill in the bed. Scattered about the garden are *Hydrangea paniculata*, *Prunus subhirtella*, a single *Cercis canadensis* 'Forest Pansy', and various vines and perennials.

BEFORE:

A sea of concrete in a rigid setting. Removing the concrete and repaving the area was cost prohibitive.

An integral part of the design and arising from it, this informal pool harmonizes with the overall composition while contributing the contrasting element of water.

A relatively inexpensive solution was brought to bear in creating an environment of graceful motion within an urban setting, complete with a small water feature at the heart of it all.

Curving planters and a water garden transform a static site into a graceful,
rhythmic symphony in brick. Shown here just after completion, vines will
soon cover the cedar fence and spill over the planter walls.

3

Raised, Formal Fountains

A Fountain Court

Site condition

This is the same site as the one discussed in A Walled Garden with Informal Fish Pool (see chapter 1), as this landscape also contains an *informal* pond in the front of the garden. In this chapter, however, we are concerned with the rear area of the property where the formal fountain is located.

The site was enclosed on three sides by a tall brick wall; the fourth side opened towards the home. Originally, a small patio was situated at this far end of the garden with just enough room for a table and chairs, but there was no order or organization to the area and no room for anything else. Although a great many plants grew here, the owner felt little pleasure in being in this part of the garden. We had decided to divide this long rectangular garden into three interconnected rooms, the far end being the formal room and clearly distinct from the decidedly informal aspect of the other two areas. After clearing this rear portion of the plants and small patio, I had an area that was open to any manner of development.

Site design

The enclosing walls lent themselves well to a formal motif and the rear wall was the perfect spot for a fountain. This formal court would be somewhat hidden from the rest of the garden and could be approached by way of an arbor and a pergola. Our intent was to create a sanctuary for private contemplation and serious thought.

The entrance to the pergola, which connects the alcove room to the fountain court, is hidden from both the informal garden and the alcove. Only by following the paved path does one discover the arched entry that is at right angles to the longest axis and offset on the right. As the plants growing on and around the pergola mature, the fountain court will become a secret sanctuary.

A person stepping through the pergola makes a right turn and stands, dead center of the fountain court, facing the lion fountain. To the person's back is the screen of vine-clad wrought iron, which encloses the formal court on the fourth side and ensures privacy. This is the moment of introduction into the fountain court and from where it can be taken in as a whole. The

BEFORE:

The far end of the garden awaiting development into a formal garden room.

The completed patio, planters, and pool
before the lion mask is mounted.

slight step down into the court heightens the sense that a room of a very different kind and a very definite purpose is now being entered.

To generate the symmetry a formal garden of this sort demands, I divided the room along its long axis with each side a mirror image of the other. The pattern in the paving stones, the planters, each side of the lion mask, and the semicircular basin on one side of the axis are identical to those on the opposite side. The iron work capping the rear wall echoes the arch of the basin, and with the vines growing on it, it carries the garden upward and also screens out unwanted views.

Water feature design

It would have been possible to extend the symmetry of this garden into the cross axis and to have placed the water garden in the center of the patio, but that would have taken up too much living space. In this finished design, there is abundant planting, a nicely sized water feature, and a lot of open area. Additionally, the wall fountain flowing into a basin is particularly fitting in the formal court and lends elegance to the setting.

The raised pool is in scale with the planters flanking it and I left a small space on either side of the pool for planting. This arrangement both hides the electrical outlet (for the pump) and frames the water feature with two vertical columns of rocky mountain juniper (*Juniperus scopulorum*). The

The lion fountain.

fountain is the same height as the planters—approximately eighteen inches—and is a good seating height. The lion mask was placed at a height that provided maximum visual effect and minimal splash; too much splash would quickly drain the pool.

Planting

Weeping or flowering cherries (*Prunus subhirtella* 'Pendula') command the four corners and will soon form an arching bower between themselves, screening out surrounding buildings. Beneath the trees are rhododendron hybrids chosen for their neat, compact habit and evergreen quality. At ground level is *Gaultheria procumbens*, a neat, glossy groundcover above which rise various irises. In the background are *Hydrangea macrophylla* 'Mariesii', which bring light and seasonal color in a range of beautiful blues. Various annuals complete the planters. Between the planters in the beds behind the benches are *Clematis* 'Jackmanii', *Liriope spicata* 'Silver Dragon', two cultivars of heucherella, and *Deutzia gracillis* 'Nikko'.

The last "room" of the garden was made into a formal sanctum arranged symmetrically along the garden's primary axis with a lion mask fountain on the center of the end wall that pours into a half-round pool. This room is lowered several inches to heighten the sense of awareness upon entering. To

Entrance to the fountain court. Wisteria will cover the decorative wrought iron atop the wall, screening out the neighboring buildings.

FORMAL, INFORMAL, AND HOW WE FEEL

A symmetrically formal environment is a controlling influence that will have a sobering, restraining effect upon us mentally and emotionally. Formal layouts have often been employed in houses of worship with the hope that abolishing the frivolous would also help to elevate and purify.

Symmetrical formality is also appropriate in a garden. However, the intent is to elevate and lighten the spirit rather than to constrain. For thousands of years, curves, water, and ornamental detail have been used to ease the restraining effect of a symmetrical environment and to make it more suited to an outdoor, garden experience without abandoning the potential for spiritual elevation. Curved lines are feminine, softer, and, like water, convey a feeling of gentle cheerfulness. They temper the effect of structure and allow the spirit to be in harmony, imbued with a sense of freedom. The ornamental detailing with, in this case, the inlaid stone in the planters and the patio, the lion mask itself, and the decorative wrought iron all add a richness that further modifies the severity of symmetry.

alleviate the severity of a formal arrangement, the planters and pool were made with curves and ornamented with light-colored river stones inset into the brick on the faces and tops of the planters and water garden and into the paving. Wrought iron in graceful curves atop the walls further lightens the atmosphere and provides growing areas for the various flowering vines. Four weeping cherries accent each corner and will provide a leafy, flowering bower to further enclose the garden. As the wisteria covers the pergola (one passes through it to enter the fountain court), this room will become a complete sanctuary, isolated from the rest of the world, so encouraging an elevated yet light-hearted mood for peaceful contemplation or quiet gatherings.

A Raised, Formal Fountain of Elegance

Site condition

No images are available of this site before its transformation but it was a typical urban setting with nothing much to say for itself: rectangular, confined, and uninteresting. The typical layout for gardens in this area included a raised bed in the center, narrow, concrete walks around three sides, and raised, narrow beds along the remaining side and rear. These gardens were rarely made usable but instead seem to have been designed for growing as many plants as possible, much as today's small urban and suburban gardens in Europe are devoted largely to vegetable growing.

Site design

The genius of this design is in the rear wall with its arching top and windows. They set the stage for the rest of the garden, which would appear far more ordinary without them. These design details lend an elegance and a grandeur to the garden and, through careful attention to balance and harmony, makes it possible to include the brick and stone patio, the multilevel brick and stone planters, the pentagonal water garden and planter, and the various sculptures.

Built across this and the adjoining property, the wall is off center of the garden. However, it does not appear that way. Why is this? Several factors are involved here: The garden is asymmetrical along both axes and does not attempt to balance symmetrically with the wall; if it did, the entire garden would be confusing and quite unsatisfying. Although the wall is weighted to the right, the garden is weighted to the left, and a balance is struck within this asymmetrical arrangement. Finally, a very clever device was employed. The metal ship has been placed just above eye level and is the point to which the eye is drawn. The ship becomes the visual center of the wall, particularly from within the garden where there is little tendency to look toward the top of the wall. In this way, the ship is the actual center of the garden, and all seems balanced along the long primary axis.

Balance was also achieved along the cross axis because of the planter that sits in the opposite corner from the fountain, the stone-topped wall on the right, and the various planted pots and the table. This garden represents a marvelous achievement of harmonious balance within an asymmetrical design.

An elegant formal garden with a raised fountain in a city setting.

Water feature design

The design for this formal fountain arose, as it always should, from the overall design of the landscape. The fountain is a natural outgrowth of everything else in the garden, from the tall rear wall through the raised beds. All is "of a piece," and the fountain mirrors the same rectangular layout and is proportional to all the other elements—it is neither too large nor too small, too high nor too low.

The water garden brings a wonderful elegance to one corner of the garden. In addition it serves as a transitional element between the otherwise overly tall rear wall, through the two levels of planters down to the patio, eliminating any abrupt leap between elevations. Finally, this garden succeeds in displaying water beautifully in a formal setting while acting as the perfect showcase for the lovely sculptures.

The fountain, nestled perfectly in a corner, is a natural outgrowth of the total design.

The tall, arching wall in the rear sets the tone for the entire landscape.

As befits a formal garden, the planting scheme relies heavily on architectural plant forms and decorative planted pots. The upright vase shape of the lilacs (*Syringa* hybrids) in the right rear is echoed in the planting of the water iris (*Iris versicolor*), the clusters of tulips and other bulbs, and the dwarf *Agapanthus* 'Peter Pan'. Common ivy (*Hedera helix*), Virginia creeper (*Parthenocissus quinquefolia*), and climbing hydrangea (*Hydrangea petiolaris*) cover the vertical surfaces. Beautiful color harmonies (mauve and purple, purple and red) have been achieved throughout the garden, as have striking contrasts (yellow and purple, white and red), both of which add a satisfying richness to the landscape.

A large, arching brick wall sets the theme of elegant grandeur in the garden and provides the balance—and backdrop—to an asymmetrically formal landscape rich in harmonizing details. The raised fountain is an integral component of the entire garden, contributing in every way to the overall design of formal elegance.

A Formal Pool in an Urban Oasis

Site condition

A concrete tile patio surrounded on three sides by narrow, straight planting beds made this garden look and feel uninhabitable. There was enough space to allow the area to be used but there was nothing inviting to make one want to be there. This was owing in part to the materials dominating the space— the overly stained red fence, the concrete edging and tiles, and the rectilinear arrangement. There was no charm or grace or warmth, and so the area looked even smaller than its actual dimensions of seventeen by sixteen feet.

Site design

Although a formal design would have worked just fine here—provided there was ample planting—the owners wanted a relaxed atmosphere imbued with a quality of sophistication. They also agreed that a small ornamental display of water would contribute to the overall atmosphere desired.

As is so often the case in these small, rectangular plots, curves, here in the brick planters and fountain, provided the desired softness and sense of motion. Inlaid blue and green tiles added brightness and a touch of elegance. Swerving the walls inward and outward in some places close to the property line and in others further away maximized both planting and living areas. Where the wall curves away from the boundary line, there was room for abundant planting, and where the walls curve in toward the property line, space becomes available for outdoor living.

The curves of the walls bring a flowing motion and help expand the sense of spaciousness with their multiple ins and outs, and the height also helps with this. Slightly lower than is normally found, the walls are yet a suitable height for seating, eliminating the need for clusters of chairs for informal gatherings.

In addition to the flowing walls, lattice atop the two side fences and a new rear fence adds airiness and light. In time the lattices will be covered with flowering vines, so providing screening in a manner delightfully suited to the overall design motif. The irregular flagging with flowing joints is also in keeping with the free-form layout of the garden.

The final component of this site design is the island within the patio that is planted in bamboo and variegated hydrangea. Not only does this planter

BEFORE:

This tiny urban plot seemed to hold little potential for a water feature.

A small, rectangular space was transformed into a graceful garden filled with motion and light.

An irregular planter line permits maximum open living area while still allowing for abundant planting.

The raised fountain is both a continuation of the walls and an ornament within the garden.

add a touch of interest and surprise, as the garden is half hidden until one steps fully into it, but it also screens the house for those in the garden, softening the entire scene.

Water feature design

The semicircular water garden was designed as a continuation of the curvy lines of the retaining walls. Placed exactly in the garden's center, it serves as a focal point that provides visual stability within the flowing motion. The line of the walls and colored tiles is repeated in the rear wall of the fountain, bringing unity to the entire vignette.

Planting

The planting scheme was chosen for its ability to bring lightness, brightness, and textural richness to the garden, with variegated, glossy, and finely textured foliage predominating. An upright flowering cherry (*Prunus serrulata* 'Kwanzan') forms a canopy in the far left corner and screens out neighboring buildings. Several ferns such as *Adiantum* and *Athyrium*, plants of *Euonymus fortunei*, *Hydrangea macrophylla* 'Mariesii', *Hypericum* 'Hidcote', *Skimmia japonica*, and various *Rhododendron* hybrids and grasses all grow beneath the canopy. (The grasses ultimately failed, however, because of inadequate light.) The bamboo is contained in a masonry planter that extends eighteen inches below grade, thus containing the otherwise invasive roots.

ONE OF THE MANY FUNCTIONS OF A GARDEN

Gardens have many roles, not least of which is to provide an environment that is imbued with the vital qualities lacking in so many of our daily experiences. We live and work in rectangular spaces and, if in the city, we are surrounded by hard and heavy man-made materials that tower threateningly over us. Were our cities made of buildings sculpted into organic forms and endowed with hanging gardens and, say, flowing water; if, in other words, our cities gave us the experience of being in a garden, then we would need gardens less in our private lives. Gardens, especially those in a city, need to be free of the qualities that characterize city life; they rarely are, however. Gardens need curves, plants, and moving water if they are to serve as palliatives to the less agreeable aspects of the workaday world.

THE MEANING OF LINE AND THE IMPORTANCE OF MATERIALS

Rectangular flagging in this garden would have created a contrast to the lines of the walls. Such contrast might be appropriate in some designs, but here it would have destroyed the sense of harmony that the owners wanted. Brick might have been employed in some appropriate design, but brick is porous and also unsuitable for shady sites, a common characteristic of urban settings. Brick holds moisture and in shade tends to encourage the growth of undesirable moss on its surfaces, becoming slippery and, ultimately, unattractive.

An urban oasis was created with curving brick walls inlaid with blue and green tiles, a free-form arrangement of flagging for the patio, and a raised water garden that forms a continuation of the walls. The planting is light and airy, and although the entire environment has a touch of elegance, it is on the whole relaxed, casual, and inviting.

The planting brings a textural richness to the garden and helps soften the wooden fence and brickwork.

A Formal Fountain
in the Japanese Tradition

Site condition
No images are available of this site before its transformation, and nor is it possible to describe it since it was built a long time ago.

A small traditional "chozubachi" fountain makes use of stone water basins and a bamboo spout. Photo by Todd Davis.

Site design

This garden was built many years ago, and considerable manpower and care was used in placing the stones. The same approach to pool creation might be done in a private garden, but on a much smaller scale.

Water feature design

This is a quiet corner of a mature landscape laid out in traditional Japanese style. The basins, fed by the bamboo fountain that appears to tap into a water source behind the large rock, are intended to offer refreshment to the garden visitor. Such fountains are also used for ritual cleansing and are often seen in front of a temple entrance.

Aside from their functional value, the fountains are the very embodiment of serenity. The solid stone basins with their placid pool of water trickling in through the bamboo, surrounded by carefully chosen stone and plants together create a world of perfect peace. This setting is completely natural, there are no artificial elements, and the only indication of man's presence is in the beautiful, respectful craftsmanship having no elaboration or affectation.

Planting

Appropriately, plants found in Japanese gardens predominate here, including *Acer palmatum*, black pine (*Pinus nigra*), *Chamaecyparis*, spreading juniper, and various azaleas (*Rhododendron* hybrids). These plants combine beautifully with stone, and they both embody and evoke the Japanese aesthetic.

This is an old established Japanese garden in a quiet corner of a botanic garden. Such a scene, on a smaller scale, could easily adorn a private landscape. The careful placement of smaller stones and the tasteful arrangement and selection of plants are vital to the success of this garden style, but those tasks are very achievable.

A Still Pool Within a Stream of Stones

Site condition

A barren and uninviting site, this remote portion of the garden was unused and unusable. It seemed to lack potential or even a reason for being.

Site design

This is another of those long, narrow sites that are divided into several different rooms, each of which offers strong contrasts as well as pleasing harmonies with those that are adjacent. A wood deck drops down a step to a bark-mulch garden that leads through a rustic arch to a garden that is paved in river stone, gravel, and concrete pavers. It is this last room that interests us now.

A simple stone basin brings life and meaning to a simple, river-stone garden. Photo by John Glover.

HARMONY BY ASSOCIATION

Normally, harmonies and contrasts are visible or audible relationships we experience through the senses, sometimes palpably. There are, however, other levels of relationships that transcend the merely physical. For example, stone and water work well together and we experience that relationship sensorially. On still another level, we recognize that rounded, smooth stones, being in fact partly created by water, are also inseparable from water. They would not exist without the influence of water and that perception, however inchoate, makes us aware of a relationship that is fundamentally onto-logical but vital and integral to our enjoyment of this combination in the garden nonetheless.

Water feature design

It is best to view this room and the water feature together, for without the stone basin, the garden would not hold our interest and would appear quite lifeless. The stone basin is what makes the garden thoroughly pleasing and successful. At the same time, the garden provides the context for the water-garden. Although we do not realize it intellectually, we instinctively associate rounded, smooth stone with water. The water brings completion to this river-stone world and gives us a sense of fulfillment.

On a more basic level, this garden and the water garden within it are both simple creations, without pretense, and fairly free of extraneous ornament; this simplicity, too, unites them, and they are of a piece. The water basin, which is round, is in harmony with the river stones while also being a dis-tinct contrast to the prominent paving squares. This minor symphony of harmonies and contrasts works on us in a pleasurable way and makes this garden the little jewel that it is.

Planting

Bamboo on the left, an unidentified small ornamental fern in the right back-ground, and what may be an *Actinidia arguta* plant in the right foreground all provide a triangulation of vertical accents. Azaleas, ferns, ornamental grass-es, and hostas fill the intermediate and lower levels with their soft foliage.

A simple garden room was created with a distinct textural contrast to the adja-cent garden but was united by the plantings. Consisting almost exclusively of washed stone and pavers, this room has a simplicity that is beguiling. The room succeeds primarily because of the wonderful harmony and contrast pro-vided by the water-filled stone basin.

Construction Details for Raised, Formal Fountains and for Raised, Informal Pools

The raised fountain is a significantly different construction from an in-ground feature. Generally, it is more difficult to build as it requires a higher level of skill, is more costly both in terms of materials and labor, and can be a little more difficult to maintain. Nevertheless, raised fountains are within the capabilities of a couple of fit people and are well worth the effort. (Construction details for raised, informal pools were discussed in chapter 2.)

Most raised fountains will be built of block, brick, stone, or some other masonry product, but a frame can also be built of wood, for example, and be given a water-retentive shell. Here I will address the several types of raised fountains discussed in chapters 2 and 3 on raised, informal and raised, formal water features. These types include fountains built of mortared brick or block, of mortared stone, of fieldstone without mortar, and of solid stone without mortar. I will also address a few options not represented with images in this chapter or in chapter 2.

The raised mortared brick or block fountain

YOU WILL NEED: *cement, sand, brick or block, level, PVC (polyvinyl chloride), trowel, shovel, and mixing pan.*

Once the pool is marked out on the ground, excavate to below frost line. If the base of the water garden is above the frost line, freezing temperatures could heave the foundation and generate cracks and leaks.

Pour the footing from approximately three parts sand, one part portland cement, and one part gravel. You can also throw small stones and rubble into the footing as well. Let the footing cure a day or two before building up the foundation to just below grade with block. The concrete will turn from a greenish color to gray when it has cured sufficiently to lay on new mortar. It is also a good idea to apply a coating of Weldcrete or similar bonding agent for binding fresh or wet cement to newly hardened cement. Once this has dried, the block walls for the foundation can be built up.

An alternative technique to pouring a footing and then building a foundation of block on top of that involves pouring the footing as one piece to just below grade without using a block. Allow an extra day or two for the footing or foundation to dry. Once it has dried, the brick walls for the foun-

Concrete block foundation
on a concrete footing.

tain are ready to be built. Follow standard brick-masonry techniques, remembering that the primary concern with brick is that every brick is laid straight, perfectly in line with the one beneath it, and perfectly level front to back and side to side. You will also want the joints between the bricks and between the rows to be consistent throughout.

One method of building in the plumbing is to build the pipe into the walls during construction and then seal around it with a watertight caulking. Another method is to completely build the basin before applying the watertight coat, build in the plumbing up the sides of the walls, and then plaster over them so that no plumbing is visible. Either way works if done properly.

It is a good idea to make it relatively easy to remove and replace the pump. To achieve this, run a larger tube or pipe up the wall from the pump location to the outflow location and run a smaller tube, which will actually carry the water, up this larger tube. For the electric wiring, run a PVC pipe up the wall that is large enough to take the plug of the electric line and plaster over that. If it is necessary to remove the pump, the water line can be pulled through the larger tube and the electric line will be pulled through the PVC pipe without the masonry being compromised. Bear in mind that water will go up the PVC pipe, but this is not a problem as long as the pipe extends above the water line before exiting the basin and has no leaks. Use thick-walled PVC (schedule 40 or 80). As an alternative to this PVC option, the electric line can be run up a corner of the wall and laid under a loose brick above the water line. Ideally, no electric wiring or plumbing should show.

Above-ground pools are subject to greater fluctuations of water temperature, surrounded as they are by walls that are constantly affected by air temperature. These temperature fluctuations can be mitigated somewhat by digging the bottom or a portion of the bottom of the pool to below grade. Making a pump-well to below grade is also a good way to mitigate temperature fluctuations and provides an out of sight place for the pump. A fine mesh covering over the well will prevent debris from entering the pool while still allowing the water to flow through so the pump will need far less cleaning. Cleaning will be a matter of occasionally taking out the cover and rinsing it off.

Once the interior of the pool is entirely waterproof, you can, if you wish, build a retaining wall inside the pool to create a planting area. Once filled with soil, this planting area will become a bog because of the moisture seeping through the retaining wall. Alternately, it is possible to give this wall a watertight coat and have an ordinary planting bed instead. This permits plants to grow behind the fall of water, which can be quite attractive.

Pools that are above ground can be very complex if they have, for example, a drain controlled by a gate valve, one or more fountains, or inlet devices. They can have a float valve allowing the pool to automatically top off when the water level falls and they can be cleaned by a skimmer leading to an external pump. Conversely, above-ground pools can be simple with a fountain rising directly out of a pump fitted with a pre-filter or mechanical filter. As we are dealing with small features for intimate settings, I will leave the more complex features to another study.

Cement is not necessarily waterproof, which means that the watertight coating you use to ensure water retention is critical. The simplest method—and that employed by swimming-pool makers—is to mix "waterproof" cement with marble dust, which is available at many masonry supply yards. (The proportions are given on the bag of marble dust.) This mixture creates a very plastic plaster that, when troweled on, gives a smooth, waterproof surface. At least two coats are recommended.

Another waterproofing agent that is foolproof if directions are followed is a combination of materials sold under the name of Mulasticoat. A twenty-pound bag of a "scratch coat" material is mixed with forty-eight ounces of water into a pancake batter consistency, and this is rolled or brushed onto a clean, dry masonry surface and left to dry for two days. Another liquid called Mulasticoat is stirred and applied with a roller to the pool's interior. When this first coat turns from power blue to dark blue, which takes at least two hours and must not be left more than three days, a second coat is applied. After two days, you can fill the pool with water.

When building a formal fountain, keep in mind that if the walls of the basin are of a cementitious material, the basin will need to be filled and drained several times over a few weeks to leach out the lime and generate a stable pH necessary for healthy fish. You can also add a diluted muriatic acid wash to quicken the process, but this weakens the cement to some extent. Alternatively, a sealant can be brushed over the finished surface to seal the lime in.

The PVC pipe holds the water line from the pump, which permits easy pump replacement.

Raised mortared stone fountains

The footing for this mortared stone fountain is identical to that of the raised, formal and informal fountain. The differences begin at just below grade with the placement of the stone. In creating a brick fountain, you need only pay attention to building level, plumb walls, and consistent joints. With a stone fountain, you must not only place the stones with a view to creating a strong wall, but you must also choose them so they create an attractive one. For the inexperienced, achieving these objectives must be a matter of experimentation.

Begin by placing a stone where it is intended to go and see how it looks with the others. Do the grain and lines of the stone harmonize with those

Careful attention to stone selection characterizes the well-built raised stone pool.

around it? If it seems less than satisfying, try another stone. It is not uncommon to pick each stone up at least five times before finding a good "home" for it. Once the outer wall has been constructed, you can place a rubber or EPDM liner in the shell or make the shell waterproof with masonry products such as Mulasticoat or marble dust.

When building a fountain with two pools, one flowing into another, it is not necessary to use one liner for both pools as long as the lower liner is laid in first and the upper one placed over that. If the upper line is laid in first, water will flow under the lower liner and out of the pool when the upper pool becomes filled with water.

In this type of construction, the plumbing must be placed so that the water can be pumped from the lower pool back into the upper. Pipe or tubing can be built through the wall separating the two pools or out through the wall of the lower pool and in through the wall of the upper pool. Similarly, a pipe can be built up the inner wall and over the top for the electric line from the pump. This pipe will then be covered with stone. Bear in mind that water will pass up this pipe so all elbow joints must be watertight.

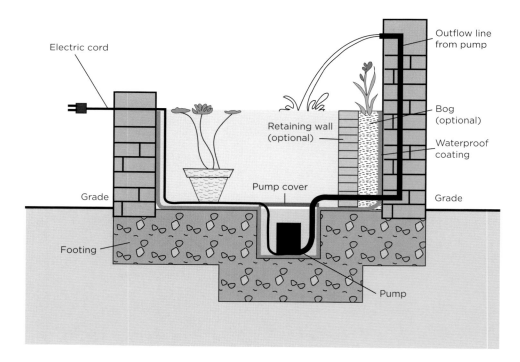

The raised mortared brick or formal fountain

If a liner is used rather than masonry waterproofing, a bulkhead fitting (a fitting that goes through the liner but is watertight) will be necessary where the pipe passes through the liner. Once the liners have been placed or the inner walls made waterproof, it is time to build the inner wall of stone. It is built in the same fashion as the outer wall. You should now build in any planters you may want. Stone planters built in the same style as the walls provide a better long-term home for water plants than do pots—and stone planters look much better.

With any kind of water feature where one pool is flowing into another, it is necessary to realize that a leak anywhere in the system will show up as a loss of water in the lower pool. This is because as long as there is water around the pump, the pump will continue supplying the upper pool with the same volume of water at the same rate. A five-hundred-gallon-per-hour pump, for example, will continue to consistently feed the upper pool at that rate minus losses due to friction and gravity. If there is a leak that drains the waterfall or if the leak is in the line or in the upper pool (unless it is a very big one), the system as a whole will be losing water; however, it is the lower pool that will show the water loss.

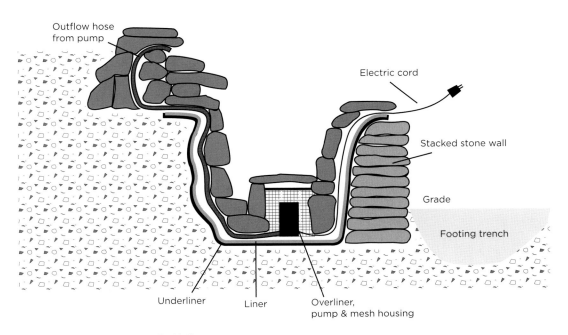

The raised, informal stone pool with liner

Raised, informal mortarless stone pool with a liner

A retaining wall of mortarless stone is built in the front of the pool (see A Natural Haven in chapter 2). The wall retains water rather than soil because of the rubber liner that is placed behind the stone and up the back side against the soil. Use standard dry wall masonry to construct the wall. (The reader is advised to consult other references for instructions on how to do this.) Run both the hose and the electric cord up the sides of the retaining wall and cover them over with the same river stone that lines the entire interior. Build a space along the sides or on the bottom of the pool to house the pump, making sure to leave enough hose and electric line free to lift the pump for cleaning, and cover it over with a thin stone on which to set a planter.

4

In-ground, Formal Fountains

In the Victorian Tradition

BEFORE:

A narrow, confined, and poorly organized space.

Once cleared of restricting elements and opened up, the true measure of the property became apparent.

Site condition

Narrow, constricted, overgrown on all sides, useless in the middle, sloping downward from end to end with an overgrown cherry tree casting deep shadows over the rear portion and yet with an air of mystery and intrigue, a hint of hidden romance from the Victorian era—such was the site before its transformation. In addition, an old, shaggy hemlock hedge on the street side and a tumbled down stone wall on the other encroached needlessly on the garden's interior space. The vague sense of Victorian romance wanted liberating and not a little polishing.

Site design

This was another site that lent itself to division because of its length and narrowness. And, as with the project A Tranquil Pool by a Peaceful Patio, an informal water garden here occupies the front area near the house while the rear portion contains the formal fountain, which in this case is an in-ground, formal pool. Because the property was sloped and because level planes are so much more inviting, the area was terraced to a height of about fourteen inches. Without terracing, the garden would have sloped through the primary outdoor living areas, which would be uncomfortable experientially and visually.

Whereas the central and primary garden room is separated from and joined to the more intimate front room by an arbor that allows easy passage back and forth, the separation between the second and third section is an arching stone wall about fourteen inches high with a single stepping stone allowing access to it. This third room, which contains the water feature, is not meant to be visited except for purposes of maintenance, and it is this literal and figurative separation that sets the area apart. We can move closer for a look into the pool's depth, the height of the step generally holds us back, and this, along with its central position, gives accent to the water garden. The fountain draws attention to the water garden, making it the focal point for the entire landscape.

Water feature design

The formality of this water feature derives from its symmetry and placement. It is on the exact center of the long axis of the entire garden and right in the

middle of the elevated plane to which it belongs. It is a perfect ellipse with an elliptically arching wall behind it from which water emerges. It is obviously man-made and yet consists of natural materials, thus embodying one of the virtues of Victorian aesthetics. This garden might be said to be a semiformal water garden, but functioning as it does as the focal point, it takes on architectural significance. The eye is drawn to it from the forefront of the landscape. In this capacity as the focal point, the water garden has the same effect a statue there would have but with the additional elements of motion and sound as water falls into water, helping to mask the street noise. The shape of the basin and the wall behind it repeat the design of the retaining wall in the foreground, so contributing to the sense of unity in the landscape.

Dividing the garden creates several usable rooms while the arbor between the first and second rooms and the raised elevation of the third create a vista through the entire garden.

Planting
The primary planting area in this portion of the property is around the water garden. Again, in keeping with the Victorian aesthetic, a woodsy planting scheme was chosen consisting of *Berberis, Cornus sericea*, mountain laurel (*Kalmia latifolia*), oak-leaf hydrangeas, and *Rhododendron maximum. Vinca minor* trails beneath this canopy and a clematis or two dangle across the face and top of the wall and grow into the shrubs.

In addition to making a bold backdrop to the water garden, these plants form a visual terminus to the garden, effectively blurring the real boundaries of the landscape, which extends another ten feet or so behind this plant grouping. Though the actual boundary of the garden is bordered by two panels of cedar lattice and a row of hemlock, plantings placed in front of this row and across only a portion of the garden's width make it unclear just where the garden ends. Such obscurity contributes to the sense of expansion, a desirable element in a small garden, and adds to the barrier against street sounds.

This third garden room is elevated above the primary garden plane and hosts an in-ground, elliptical pool edged in stone with an arching stone wall behind it. The pool's placement in the middle of a small garden area at the end of the property and at the center of the long axis of the landscape contributes to the room's formal aspect, as does its shape and elevation. Though set off from the rest of the garden as if on display, this third room is nevertheless united with the primary garden room through its arching stone wall, which repeats the shape of the wall retaining this third garden room. The room is the focal point of the entire landscape and serves, upon entrance to the garden, to draw the eye along its entire length. A variety of woodsy, flowering shrubs and vines gives the room a handsomely rustic backdrop that sets off both the stone and falling water.

An in-ground, elliptical formal pool with a raised wall brings a touch of elegance to the garden.

A Floral Fountain Court

Site condition

Here was a rectangular plot in an urban environment not unlike those spaces attached to dwellings and religious buildings in the Middle Ages that often became cloister gardens. And a cloister garden, with a few significant modifications, is what this space became.

A centrally placed fountain surrounded by planting beds that is reminiscent of a cloister garden. Photo by John Glover.

Site design

A typical cloistered garden from the Middle Ages was characterized by a pool or fountain centrally placed for the convenience of bringing water to all parts of the garden, normally one of vegetables and herbs, and by paths leading to the various planting areas. Such is the style of garden we find here. Though not used for watering the garden, the fountain is nevertheless centrally placed. The paths separate and join the various planting areas that have been made from every available space not otherwise occupied by walkways or the fountain. The result is an abundant, floral lushness with the life-giving water source as the central focal point.

This design is a splendid motif when an abundance of species, such as is found in perennial gardens or English cottage gardens, is what is wanted. Seen against the foreground of splashing water, the lavish beds look all the more appealing.

Water feature design

Though the edge of this fountain is raised a few inches above grade, it is nevertheless an in-ground pool with most of its depth set below grade. A pump forces the water up through the fountain from which the water falls back into the basin below. Such an arrangement in which the tiered metal fountain rises about four and a half feet above the pool provides maximum visual and audio effect. The cut corners of the fountain are a pleasant ornamental detail, while the slightly raised walls help create a balance with the mass of the fountain.

Planting

In the background are *Fremontodendron californicum*, California lilac (*Ceanothus*), various climbing roses, and foxgloves (*Digitalis*), while to the middle and foreground are peonies (*Paeonia*), irises, lilies, calla lilies (*Zantedeschia aethiopica*), lupins (*Lupinus*), astilbes, alliums, veronicas, lobelias, and geraniums. Around the pool are lobelias and dianthus with *Cotoneaster horizontalis* and a few lilies in the garden's corners.

An enclosed court was modeled in the style of a cloister garden but with an abundance of cheerful blossoms and an ornamental fountain in the center. With its dashing contrasts and a lush abundance of brilliant color, the garden's overall effect is of gaiety and freedom in an artfully controlled environment.

A Sunken Brick Patio Pool

Site condition

This is another of those urban settings that could have been left as is or made uneventful but instead became a pleasure garden through tasteful design. All too frequently, such sites are left as mere spaces without much in the way of ornament, providing little pleasure for the eye or body.

A simple, rectangular, in-ground pool
with a jet fountain brings life and
activity to a brick patio.
Photo by John Glover.

THE VALUE OF FORMALITY

Very few people, when contemplating a new garden, consider a formal design. Most don't think of themselves as the "formal" type, but everyone can profit from the effect of formality, and most gardens can accommodate a formal element somewhere within it, if not in the entire design. For example, a garden can be quite wild and free-form around its borders while supporting a classical formal water garden in the center, that arrangement in itself being a classically formal arrangement. Alternatively, a garden may be divided into two or more rooms (as it was with A Walled Garden with Informal Fish Pool) wherein one room is in a classically formal design. Having access to a formal arrangement that we simply behold or in which we may spend time can be elevating. Almost all of us possess an appreciation of formality, and although we may not want a garden entirely in this style, some element of formality would contribute to the beauty of many gardens and to our enjoyment of them.

Site design

The design is relatively simple and features a decorative, arching lattice fence that forms the side boundaries of a brick patio that in turn is ornamented with planted pots, a pergola, and an in-ground, centrally located water garden. The pergola is placed so that it provides maximum enjoyment of the water garden. This patio arrangement with its central water feature and nearby sitting areas is suitable to many patio gardens. It is neither difficult nor expensive to build but, as this garden shows, can be highly enjoyable.

Water feature design

The sunken pool is among the most satisfying and yet the simplest formal pools to build. It is a simple rectangle with a waterproof masonry interior. Sunken pools can also be built with liners that are made to order according to the exact size and shape wanted. The pump can be tucked away in a corner and the electric wiring laid in under the brick out of sight. In this example, the pump is hidden beneath the jet fountain. The pool supports numerous water plants, fish, and snails, which help keep the water and the sides free of algae.

Planters were built into the patio around the pool with one side left open for access. Though raised planters might have been used, they would have obscured the pool too much. The jet fountain shoots water several feet into the air, creating a misty environment in the vicinity of the pool.

Planting

In the water are yellow flags (*Iris pseudacorus*) and rough horsetail (*Equisetum hyemale*), both of which provide good vertical accents against the horizontal plane of the pool. Surrounding the pool is a mixed medley of some of the owners' favorites in no particular design. Ivy rambles about with its brightening variegation, *Lavandula stoechas* and *Campanula* grow in the foreground, and to the left are *Potentilla* species together with drifts of violets and geraniums. In pots there are cabbage trees (*Cordyline*) and heliotropes with monarda and roses in the background.

An urban rectangular plot was made into a charming patio garden with a central, in-ground pool containing a jet fountain that is surrounded by abundant plantings. A pergola placed nearby offers a shady haven from which to enjoy the pool and garden. The jet fountain here is a contemporary touch, but for a more classical look, side fountains of small animals, a small figure, or a central fountain sculpture could be used instead.

Classical Symmetry in a Formal Courtyard

Site condition

This property adjoins property to A Symphony in Brick, and like that garden, this one's layout was very rigid. It was different from the Symphony in Brick project in that a planting bed was in this property's center. Although it lacked all sense of graciousness, the potential was there. This owner, with a classically stylish home, tended to the formal, and that same elegance needed to be brought out in the garden.

Site design

Brick planters constructed in half circles with coping made of two-inch-thick, quarry-cut bluestone with flamed edges are separated from one another by cedar lattice arches that were custom-built. This same pattern is mirrored on the other side of the garden. The arches and planters lead the eye to the end of the garden, which is planted in trees and shrubs. In the garden's center is a planted bed and water garden. The symmetry of the design conveys formality, while the perfect half-circle of the planters, repeated in the arches, and the classical composition of materials provide the wanted elegance.

Water feature design

Although removing all the repaving and concrete was cost prohibitive, several feet of concrete were removed to accommodate an in-ground, rectangular pool. The interior was made water retentive with a rubber liner, but it was completely fitted with bluestone. The pool was also given a bluestone edging.

The dimensions of the pool reflect the overall dimensions of the garden, which helps integrate it. Likewise, the bluestone edging harmonizes with the planters' coping and helps unite the garden as well.

Planting

The four end planters contain *Stewartia pseudocamellia* and the two center planters contain *Oxydendrum arboreum*. Both trees take partial shade, are easily kept to a comfortable size, and retain a pleasing and manageable form. Beneath the trees are dwarf *Tsuga canadensis* 'Pendula', ivy, ferns, bleeding hearts (*Dicentra*), and a variety of bulbs and annuals.

BEFORE:

A long rectangular space held the promise of formal elegance but needed a complete rethinking of materials.

An eclectic selection of distinctively formed plants complement the formal symmetry.

Overlooking the water garden are a Japanese maple and a redbud cultivar (*Cercis canadensis* 'Forest Pansy'), while the borders are edged in azaleas and variegated forget-me-nots (*Myosotis scorpioides*). In planters are roses, holly (*Ilex*), and several clematis cultivars.

In the center of the rear planting bed and the backdrop to all this is a dwarf blue spruce (*Picea pungens* 'Glauca Bakeri'), and on both sides of that tree is a river birch. Beneath and between the spruces are rhododendrons, spireas (*Spiraea*), clematis, honeysuckles, *Hydrangea macrophylla*, and a variety of perennials and bulbs.

A cold and barren rectangular space was transformed into classical elegance through a symmetrical design and classical elements and materials. Central to the garden is the formal, in-ground pool and fish fountains.

A rectangular classical pool with stone coping and interior.

Construction Details for the In-ground, Formal Fountain

YOU WILL NEED: *shovel, long or line level, underliner, liner, and interior material.*

In this chapter I address building the in-ground, formal fountain with a flexible liner. If masonry construction is preferred, excavate as indicated in this chapter and then follow the masonry instructions from chapter 3 using either concrete block or brick.

Construction of the in-ground, formal fountain is fairly straightforward, the only difficulty being how to ensure the exactness of symmetry. It is essential, in striving for perfect symmetry, to make all phases of the construction, from the excavation to the final finishing with the interior material, as precise as possible.

It is possible to have a formal fountain's liner and the hardware for securing the corners made to exact dimensions. This custom-made option eliminates the bother of fitting the liner into the corners and trying to make it lie flat. If no final finishing material such as stone will cover the liner, it is advisable to have the liner and hardware specially made. In this example of a formal fountain, however, the pool was finished in bluestone, so an ordinary ten-foot by ten-foot liner was used and then fitted in by hand.

The formal pool is excavated as precisely as possible with straight, even sides.

Once the liner is laid in, it must be made to fit as well as possible by fold-ing pleats into it. Once that is done, the finish material can be built in.

The measurements of this pool were designed so that precut, standard-sized bluestone could cover the pool's sides and bottom in a way that made a perfect box. Holes were cut from the bottom pieces of the stone for the planter and the pump and the stones were mortared together over the liner. As a last detail, a bluestone coping was laid in mortar to provide a frame to the formal pool.

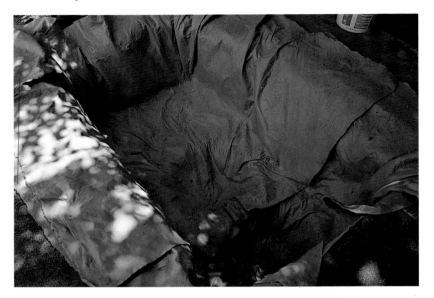

The underliner goes in before the liner to prevent damage to the liner from abrasion. Note the two depressions in the bottom; one is for a planter, the other for the pump.

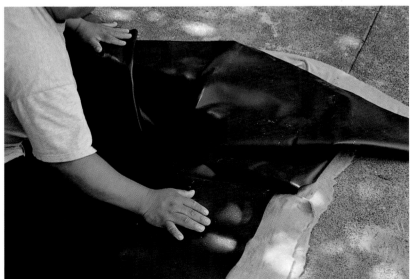

To make the liner lay flat, fold the pleats in very carefully.

5

Wall Fountains

Formal Elegance

Wall fountains are usually used to ornament existing sites that are already well designed and developed, so the site condition is not an issue. In addressing the selection and placement of wall fountains, I therefore refer to the location, fountain design, site enhancement, and planting.

A cast-lead fountain in a classical ram's head design ornamented in a festive motif. Photo by John Glover.

Location

An existing wall in an established patio garden was given a highly polished, very ornamental decoration with the inclusion of the ram's head wall fountain. Note the clean lines of the wall and classical arrangement of the clipped box and trailing ivy, all very well suited to this particular fountain.

Fountain design

The fountain is cast lead, available from a variety of foundries in the United States and in Europe. (See "Resources.") Wall fountains come in many styles, from the highly ornate to the almost gaudy, the whimsical, the extremely formal, the sedate, contemporary, humorous, and so on. The ram's head with braided beard in garland fashion indicates a classical motif, but there is also a strongly architectural element built into the design with the side and central columns. Though these columns were not strictly necessary for this fountain to be effective, they do contribute to the architectural mood of this part of the garden.

Site enhancement

Vines frame the fountain around its top and sides, while the topiary accents the architectural element of the fountain.

Planting

Ivy creates the embellishing frame around the fountain, and the topiary in clipped box (*Buxus*) is at once simple and classical.

A formal setting was elevated by adding a classically designed wall fountain to the plain, simple wall. Trailing ivy provides an excellent frame to the fountain while a clipped box accents the front of the fountain. This latter element might be more effective if only the lower tier of the plant were there; as it is, it seems to interfere with the fountain and will continue to do so as it grows.

A Lion's Leafy Den

Location
A corner of the garden that would otherwise go unused and possibly unappreciated becomes, with the inclusion of this lion-mask wall fountain and the accompanying planting, a garden showpiece and a thoroughly delightful vignette.

Fountain design
A relatively ornate mask fountain of a serious nature is intended to be impressive both in its overall design, which is formally elegant, and in the visual impact created by the lion's head itself. There is nothing whimsical about this wall fountain.

Site embellishment
The fountain is made both more impressive and more beautiful by the verdant surroundings. The vine encasement is especially effective; following the arch of the fountain as it does, it softens while it ornaments.

Planting
Creeping fig (*Ficus pumila*) creates the lion's "mane" and is perfectly suited to the garden situation. Slender sweet flags (*Acorus gramineus*), calla lilies, ivy, and other creeping plants help contribute to the appropriate jungly quality of the setting.

A lion-mask fountain tucked into a quiet corner that is heavily planted creates a captivating setting of considerable beauty. Such a creation, because of its unique beauty, becomes a place to visit, a reason to wander through the garden.

This lion mask in cast stone is richly embellished in a jungle of flora and foliage. Photo by John Glover.

A Little Niche of Formal Elegance

A fountain of classical design mounted to the wall that maintains a garden feel. Photo by John Glover.

Location

Though this fountain could have been mounted to the wall, it is instead placed in front of it and slightly elevated to give it more "place of prominence." Normally a fountain like this would be placed still higher up on a wall to allow the face to be more easily viewed but it works well in this location too.

Fountain design

This lead fountain is entirely self-contained, requiring only a nearby outlet. It is of classical design with just enough ornamental detail to give it an elegant look while maintaining a garden feel. Note that the top of the fountain is intended to be planted.

Site embellishment

This pleasant but plain brick wall was elevated in this little niche to the level of formal elegance by the addition of the water feature and lattice. It is remarkable how much such a simple device can transform the look of a small space. This spot has been made a focal point of considerable beauty and appeal, so it was not necessary to carry the latticework the extent of the wall. The abundant planting all around the fountain softens it and keeps it contained in a natural setting.

Planting

The purple foliage of *Heuchera* 'Palace Purple' in the foreground are edged on the inside with the brightly contrasting foliage and blossom of a senecio plant, on the outside with blue columbine (an *Aquilegia* hybrid), and to the rear with dwarf clipped box. A hybrid lily forms a vertical accent to both sides (it is only visible here on the right), while ivy creeps up the lattice behind the water feature. The large-leaved vine *Vitis* 'Brant' forms a pleasant contrast to all the fine detail of foliage and flower.

The addition of the lattice and the wall fountain transformed this little place along a simple wall into a focal point of considerable beauty and elegance. A planting pallet rich in color and texture completed the picture.

An Urban Garden with a Private Pergola

Location

An open, empty backyard in the city was in desperate need of a gracious enclosure and usable space. In a yard such as this, one not only feels entirely exposed to the gaze of neighbors but also overwhelmed by unwanted views of neighboring buildings. Offering nothing in the way of pleasurable experiences or charming scenes, it needed to become a garden and a landscape. In the course of designing the entire garden, I was determined that a fountain should be placed in the center of the rear wall where it could be enjoyed from within the garden as well as from within the pergola.

Fountain design

This fountain was designed as three separate components: a fountain, a spill basin, and a bottom pool. This arrangement permitted the right amount of ornamentation—neither too much nor or too little—but it required that the plumbing and electrical wiring be built into the wall, lest the view of them detract from the beauty of the fountain.

Site embellishment

The fountain was designed as an integral component of the landscape, ornamenting the otherwise plain basic brick wall and providing the refreshing sight and sound of falling water. Because of its location, it is enjoyed from within the garden proper and also from the private pergola. The garden was made into three distinct areas, each offering its own uses and pleasures. The front or entry garden exists primarily for the enjoyment of gardening in raised planters and in-ground beds. This leads through an arbor to the second room, which is large enough for a table and about six chairs for outdoor dining. From this room you can enter the garden room or pergola. This pergola is built of the same brick as the wall, and the planters are inset with colored glass blocks. The upper walls of the pergola are made of cedar lattice, posts, and beams, and the structure features waterproof cedar storage benches. The pergola, once covered in vines, will offer some privacy in an urban environment.

BEFORE:

An empty urban lot in need of becoming a garden.

A wall fountain of three separate components with the utilities built into the wall brings the right degree of ornamentation to the setting.

Planting

Near the fountain there are climbing hydrangeas (*Hydrangea anomala* subsp. *petiolaris*), fast growing knotweeds (*Polygonum*), and clematis hybrids. To the left is *Hydrangea paniculata* 'Kyushu'. Climbing hydrangeas soften the brick wall, and the knotweeds and clematis both ornament and shade the pergola. The hydrangea lends a graceful, weeping element to the otherwise linear boundary.

A typically barren, open urban yard was turned into a gracious landscape comprising several garden rooms, a pergola with cedar storage benches, and arched windows and entryway. The wall fountain at the center of the rear wall provides pleasure to all parts of the garden.

The same yard, dispossessed of disagreeable elements and rendered an elegant setting with a wall fountain.

Construction Details for the Wall Fountain

YOU WILL NEED: *the fountain, a drill, screws and driver, and tubing.*

A wall fountain usually consists of a mask, rosette, or other ornamental device from which water emerges as a small stream flowing into a basin. The basin contains a built-in pump from which water will be pumped back to the mask. Alternatively, the water may fall into another basin or a series of basins, recirculating from the bottom basin back where the pump is, to the top of the fountain. The wall fountain that is easiest to install is the self-contained unit whereby the basin and fountain are all one piece. If the basin and fountain are separate pieces, the water line from the basin to the fountain must be hidden from view or made ornamental some way.

Wall fountains are generally placed on existing walls. If the basin is a separate component from the fountain, the chief difficulty in placing wall fountains is hiding the plumbing and the electric wires. It is particularly difficult if access to the back of the wall is not possible or if the lines cannot show in the back. In this case, the only way to effectively hide the plumbing and electrical parts is to run them up the inside of the wall. In a brick wall, this will require removing enough bricks from the bottom basin to the outflow so that a tube will fit into the wall. It is best if the tube is large enough to contain the smaller tube that will carry the water. Similarly, bricks will need to be removed and a tube inserted into the opening through which the electric cord can be pulled. The bricks that have been removed will need to be cut to a lesser thickness before being replaced in the wall. If the wall is not of brick but of some other masonry material, a section can be cut out with an angle grinder and then mortared back over once the lines are in place.

If you can access the rear of the wall, simply drill two holes for the water line and two for the electric line. Drill first the hole where the mask or rosette will go. Suspend a plumb line from this hole to mark where the basin should go and drill another hole behind the basin. From the front of the wall, drop a string through the top hole down the back of the wall and pull it through the bottom hole. Tie the string to a tube of the appropriate size and, from the back of the wall, pull the string up and through the top hole to the front of the wall. Be sure to leave enough tubing to attach to the outflow device, which could be a mask, spout, or something else. The extra tubing can be cut off later once the correct length is determined. Drill holes for the electric wiring that are large enough to get the plug through. Drop a string from the top hole to the bottom, pull it through the bottom hole, tie the plug to the top of the string, and pull the string from the bottom so that the plug comes through the wall at the bottom. Be sure there is enough electric cord pulled through to reach the outlet.

It is important to place the outflow and the basin close enough to one another so that there is not too much splash. Even a fairly small amount of water splashing out will drain the bottom basin and eventually burn out the pump. Fountains that are supplied with pumps normally have a flow adjustment mechanism on the pump, so getting the proper volume and rate of discharge simply requires adjusting the outflow on the pump.

6

Streams

A Musical Stream

Site condition
This is the same site discussed in chapter 2, Raised Pools in a Public Place. In that chapter we were concerned with the raised pools; here we focus on the stream that connects them.

Site design
The intent of this landscape design was to create a miniature world of grace, peace, and harmony. The hope was that the resulting environment would have a positive, uplifting effect, that it would possess a certain vitality and integrity, and that it would be a pleasant place to be in. Everything in the design, from the curving walkways to the secluded seating areas, the plantings, and especially the moving water, was intended to contribute to this effect.

Water feature design
The stream was the key element to this garden. It, above all, established the lyrical, idyllic quality that was intended to predominate and set the tone. The stream originates where the large, raised fountain spills over a smooth boulder into the head of the stream and then winds down through the garden, roughly paralleling the walkway to the front door. It was kept shallow to generate a faster flow and made to look as natural as possible.

Planting
Plants along the stream were selected both for their visual contribution to a natural environment and for their ability to keep children from playing in the stream. There are prickly creeping juniper, *Berberis thunbergii* 'Atropurpurea', *B. thunbergii* 'Crimson Pygmy', and *B. julianae*. Plants that soften while contributing to the meadow motif include Chinese pennisetum (*Pennisetum alopecuroides*), *Caryopteris* ×*clandonensis*, and *Houttuynia cordata*, which will take a lot of abuse. *Euonymus fortunei* and a variety of creeping perennials tucked into pockets among the river stone will, in time, completely soften the rocky stream margins.

BEFORE:

The site at the early stages as the author clears and excavates it.

The river-stone coping on the wall is also part of the stream, helping to bring unity to the setting.

The stream is the understated but key focal point of this school of music's entire landscape. Joining the upper area of the garden with the lower, it at once reiterates and embodies the school's purpose—the creation of music—in a gracious setting.

THE INESTIMABLE IMPORTANCE OF UNITY

It is crucial that a natural stream in an urban environment be integrated thoroughly with its surroundings. This entire landscape is an organic composition comprised for the most part of natural materials and curving lines. A stream was not out of keeping here, and it was further integrated with the landscape through its natural-looking borders of river boulders and appropriate plants. Particularly important to the sense of unity was the lower wall, which runs just beneath and alongside the stream; it was capped, not in Brownstone like the other wall, but in river boulders, some of which are also part of the streambed.

The planted stream featuring plants that blend in naturally with the setting, enhancing the sense of overall harmony.

Flowing Water in a Brooklyn Backyard

Site condition

As the before photo shows, this was a garden patio that had nothing particularly wrong with it; it was simply uninteresting. The owners wanted a
change; they craved a quiet, informal setting that would delight the senses
in a peaceful way while also providing a touch of excitement. Their wish may
seem contradictory but in actuality, a stream can offer just that combination.
It is peaceful, with the gentle flow of water, the slight swaying of water
plants, the lazy gliding of fish. Having a stream in your own backyard—that
is exciting. In addition to the flora and fauna that you provide, a stream will
attracts birds, butterflies, frogs, and other gentle creatures; it becomes a
habitat that, although constant, is also always changing, that is a living part
of your world.

Site design

There was plenty of space for a stream without it encroaching on the living
area as long as it wrapped the edge of the patio. Since the natural headwater
was in the far left corner of the garden (where it was also out of the way yet
very visible), the stream could meander beneath the hemlock, skirt the right
edge of the property, and terminate in a small pool that swells slightly
toward the middle of the patio.

Water feature design

The upper pool, where the water emerges, is built in the style of a natural
spring, and the water flows from a stone wall into the pool. A waterfall was
built so that as the water nears the top of the stone basin it spills out and
flows over a series of falls and then into the stream. The stream widens and
narrows along its length as it meanders around the patio edge. (A narrow
portion of the patio was removed to construct the stream.) The water is
pumped underground back from the small pool at the end of the stream and
along the outside edge of the stream to the upper pool, where it reappears
as the flow into the basin.

Only a small flow was appropriate for a pool this size, but because the
water tended to become too still in the middle of the stream, an additional

An upper pool flows into a stream that skirts the patio edge.

pump was installed in this middle section. The pump simply recirculates the water, creating a current to help move the water along. The pump was added purely for the aesthetic value of movement; gravity allows the water to flow from top to bottom quite adequately without the need for an additional pump.

As is always the case in creating the natural stream, stone type and stone placement are vital. The stones should be of the same kind as those found in and along streams, especially if they will be used in the stream, and they should be placed and arranged in as realistic a manner as possible. This can be especially difficult when building a stream where no stream has ever been, but every effort to simulate nature will make the difference between a stream that really looks good and one that appears completely contrived.

GOOD IS GOOD, BEAUTFUL IS BETTER

All too often we have a garden or patio that seems fine; it works, we're able to use it, it's good. But with a little imagination, that same place, one that we see or visit often, could become beautiful, and in so doing, could add significantly to the quality of our lives.

Planting groups can be vivified by distinct harmonies or contrasts; simply changing a couple of plants is often all that is needed. A walkway can become enchanting if it is supplemented with an arbor, and a patio can be livened up with the addition of a water feature.

Planting

Cotoneaster horizontalis and *Euonymus fortunei* spread along the upper pool's ledge and climb down over the wall. On the other side of the waterfall an *Acer palmatum* var. *dissectum* arches over the trickling cascades. A Chinese wisteria (*Wisteria sinensis*) climbs up the Eastern hemlock (*Tsuga canadensis*) with tufts of *Liriope muscari* in a grassy bed beneath an azalea (*Rhododendron* 'Delaware Valley White'). Behind is a well-formed Japanese andromeda (*Pieris japonica*), which provides a picturesque backdrop to this quiet vignette. Clumps of grasses such as *Miscanthus*, daylilies, irises, dianthus, and various bulbs line the stream's edge.

An ordinary rear patio garden was transformed into a haven of natural beauty for easy enjoyment. An upper pool spills over a small waterfall into a stream and then into a small lower pool. The careful selection and placement of stones and the planting of appropriate, naturalizing plants transform the garden into something that could have been stolen from a woodland and placed in an urban environment.

When the plants have matured, the stream and its surrounds are luxuriantly softened.

A cut-leaf maple (*Acer palmatum* var. *dissectum*) forms a graceful canopy over the stream, providing shade for fish and plants.

A Wild, Romantic Ruins with a Stream Running Through

Site condition

This is the kind of site a designer loves to be given, an empty, open space with a hidden garden just waiting to be discovered and developed. It was a space in which most anything could be done—but what should be done? The site itself offered few clues as to how best to bring out its potential. It was raw, plain, and bereft of any inspiring element.

As it happened, inspiration came from the owners: they wanted "a wild, romantic tangle." They had no idea just how that idea might be made manifest, but that is what designers are for, to understand the owners' wants and tastes and to determine how best to express them in a living landscape.

Site design

The clients' intense attraction to ancient Greece and Rome, along with their request for wild romance, led to the creation of an overgrown, ancient ruins with an artesian well that spills water into a stream that in turn terminates in a small pond containing a wide variety of flora and fauna.

To generate dimensionality beyond the existing, flat plain, six hundred cubic feet of soil and about four tons of moss rock were brought in. Many of these stones were used to retain in a rough, structural fashion the various elevations that were sculpted out of the new soil embankments, the embankments being reminiscent of the stones of an ancient ruin. This provided a starting framework.

The stream was designed as the primary element of this landscape, one of vigor and life around which the garden thrives. It originates near the upper right-hand corner of the garden and flows to the garden's lower left, leaving room on the right for planting and for a bench beneath the weeping cherry. On the left is a gravel path, which traverses the garden. Beyond the path and to its right is an abundance of foliage and flower, as well as another nook, bench, and weeping cherry. A stone bridge was built at the patio's gated entry into the garden where the stream cuts across the garden. The stream flows beneath the bridge and into the bottom pool.

The patio area in this setting is the primary living space and the main vantage point from which the garden is enjoyed. The garden, therefore, is not meant for living in but for walking through, admiring, sitting in (the

BEFORE:

An empty space waiting for its potential to be discovered.

IF IT CAN BE IMAGINED, IT CAN BE

When considering the possibilities for a garden, it is useful to abandon standard notions and commonplace paradigms. Just because the space is small and in an urban environment does not mean it has to be an ordinary city garden with a patio, raised beds, and shade tolerant shrubs. Similarly, a suburban garden does not have to have a lawn and foundation planting with the overly obvious "specimen" tree. Just about anything is possible for any garden, and what is created should be dictated by personal taste and an imagination that tends toward the beautiful.

A wild, romantic tangle with artesian well, stream, koi pool, and garden.

The garden as seen from the sculpture court patio.

flowering cherries, for example, provide a perfect canopy), plant tending, and losing oneself in during daily excursions into a world quite unlike anything else around.

Water feature design

It was not possible to place by hand the fifteen-hundred-pound moss rock that would form the head of the stream, at least not with any degree of precision. A modular machine that could be dismantled and brought in and out of the property had been specifically designed for this project to allow stones to be precisely placed during the building of the artesian well. An artesian well is one in which underground water flows naturally to the surface, often through rock fissures, forming a natural basin and then spilling out to create and sustain a stream. That was the kind of feature I needed to realize the owners' hopes for a wild, romantic tangle.

Waterfall design and construction for this project and in general are addressed in detail in chapter 9. In this chapter we are concerned with the stream.

It is difficult to appreciate merely from looking at pictures how a garden like this becomes such a thoroughly convincing reality. If the garden is well made (meaning that it is a unified environment imbued with ambience and replete with a keen attention to nature's details), it has the capacity to transport the visitor with an experience that is difficult to attain in the wild, let alone in an urban backyard.

The artesian well required the stones to be carefully and exactly placed to best simulate nature.

Planting

Plant enthusiasts will spend some time here sorting through the many genera and species that make up this gardens flora. In keeping with the theme of tangle and romance, plants were selected, for the most part, for their natural, wild, or romantic attributes. Some of those plants include *Aralia elata* 'Variegata', red-twigged dogwoods (*Cornus alba* 'Elegantissima'), berberis, Eastern flowering dogwoods (*Cornus florida*), climbing red roses (*Rosa* 'Don Juan'), weeping cherries (*Prunus subhirtella* 'Pendula'), Japanese anemones (*Anemone hupehensis*), dicentras, irises, daphnes, Chinese wisterias (*Wisteria sinensis*), sweet woodruffs (*Galium odoratum*), lilacs (*Syringa* species), and viburnums such as *Viburnum ×burkwoodii*. There are also oak-leaf hydrangeas (*Hydrangea quercifolia* 'Alice'), hostas, fragrant azaleas (*Rhododendron* 'Weston's Innocence'), pennisetums, columbines (*Aquilegia* hybrids), and clematis. Other plants that might normally be considered more formal but that in this environment contributed to a pagan, woodsy feel include unclipped boxwoods (*Buxus microphylla* var. *koreana* × *Buxus sempervirens*),

Water from the artesian well spills over a fall into the stream that meanders through the property.

Japanese cedar, leyland cypress (×*Cupressocyparis leylandii*), *Ilex* ×*meserveae*, and *Hydrangea macrophylla*. Ferns, bracken, tufts of campanula, violets, and pansies (the owners love their out-of-sync splashes of color) are equally well suited to the wild romance of this garden.

The theme the owners specified gave rise to the creation of an overgrown, ancient-looking ruins with stone that was arranged in a rough structural fashion and that retained different elevations of soil. The stream originates in an artesian well and winds through the garden, terminating in a lower pond that is filled with varying flora and fauna and presided over by a gargoyle looking out at this fantastic scene with its plethora of woodsy, pagan, romantic plants. A path drifts through the garden from which visitors can see pieces of statuary and the "ruins" of ancient buildings scattered about. Two benches on opposite sides of the garden invite the visitor to become lost within this wonderful, captivating world.

An astonishing array of species in harmonious disarray.

Construction Details for the Liner-Built Stream

YOU WILL NEED: *liner, underliner, tubing, and level.*

Although streams can be made of concrete, it is too massive an undertaking for the average homeowner or even the average pond builder, both in terms of technical complexity and labor. I therefore do not address it in this book. I also do not discuss the installation of prefabricated stream shells because they are far too limiting in terms of size and shape and because they possess no advantages over the liner-built stream.

If you have the space—you don't need much; fifteen feet will do—a stream can be a thoroughly delightful element in a landscape. The best place for a stream is on a slight slope (the streambed itself, however, will not slope) where it can be easily seen and enjoyed and where it gets as much light as possible. If you are building on a strong slope, create steps separating lengths of nearly level watercourse. Natural streams do not appear to slope; rather, they flow over an apparently even plane, then drop through a fall or series of falls to the next, lower plane.

Construction of the stream is much the same as it is for an informal pool. A stream can be thought of as a shallow, elongated pool that usually connects a higher elevation water source to a lower elevation pond. The pump goes in the lower pond and the return hose, which is buried underground, runs along the streambed to the upper source.

In laying out the stream, give it some curves but do not exaggerate them. Where the stream bends, widen it, and when the liner is in place, set a stone or stones on the inside bend as if they are the cause of the deflected watercourse. To generate rapids, make the stream more shallow or more narrow—or both. It is best to make these adjustments in the ground before the liner is in place. It can then be enhanced with small stones placed inside the stream over the liner. Doing so is often advantageous in the middle or toward the end of a stream if the water flow is not sluggish.

Unless you plan to create a torrent using a large pump, make the stream shallow, from three to eight inches or so, and give the sides a gradual, not steep, slope. Gently sloping banks make it easy to hide the liner with washed river gravel and small stones. You can also build in planting areas along the stream's sides for bog plants, greatly adding to the naturalness of the

The stream, once dug, is ready to receive the underliner and liner. Note that it is wider where it bends.

stream. Keep in mind, however, that plants use water, and the more plants there are drawing from the stream, the more you will need to top off of the stream system.

Before laying in the liner, you would be well served to first lay in an underliner to prevent holes and tears from forming in the liner. It is also useful, for the same reason, to have at least two pairs of hands to drop the liner into place so that you don't have to drag it over the ground.

The liner for the stream can be a continuation of that used for the upper water source and it can also continue to be that of the lower water source. The liner, then, need not be all one piece. As long as the upper pool liner lies over the stream liner, and as long as the stream liner extends above the water line and beneath the upper liner, there will be no water loss. At the stream's lower end, the stream liner must lie over the bottom pool liner with the bottom pool liner pulled above the water line. When laying in the liner, be sure to leave excess liner at any significant elevation changes. You will need the extra material when building the cascades at these elevation points.

Making the stream look natural is the tricky part. One aspect of the difficulty is how to get the water to flow over, not under, the rocks, especially where the cascades have been built. If you just place rocks in the stream without working with the technique I describe, you will wonder where all the water has gone. You will see plenty of water coming over the falls, but the stream will not reflect this because the water will be running under the stones rather than cascading over them. Maintaining a strong stream flow is the reason you left extra liner at the points of elevation change. This is where the extra liner at the elevation changes comes in.

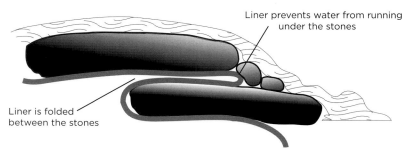

Liner prevents water from running under the stones

Liner is folded between the stones

The topmost cascade must have the liner folded over the stone.

As shown above, the top-most stone is inserted into a fold in the excess liner so that the liner covers the front half of the stone. That stone is given a very slight tilt forward. Once the stone with the liner over it is set, any stones placed under that stone and tilted slightly forward will carry the water forward into the stream, negating the need for more work with the liner. Smaller stones are then placed on top of and in front of the liner to hide it.

Water from the upper source fills up behind the top stone, flows up over the liner, then over and off the top stone. Appropriate stones well placed both in and around the stream will do much to further the appearance of a natural stream, as will turf, washed gravel, or ground cover planted up to the liner's edge and rounded, washed stone that covers the length of the liner. Planting groups randomly dispersed along the length of the stream as well as a few plants in the water itself will round out the picture.

Another technique you can use to ensure that water flows over the stones and not under the stones involves cementing the joints to seal them, thereby forcing the water to stay on the surface. The problem with using cement is that lime leaches from it, which raises the pH of the water. However, this is a short-term problem. Another potential drawback with cement is that it may crack in colder climates, creating leaks. This can be prevented by using

Testing the waterfall.

chicken wire in the cement to give it binding strength, but this process entails considerable labor.

You will need a larger pump with a stream than a pool of equal volume to compensate for the friction from the length of the return line and for the elevation difference between the bottom of the lower pool and the entry point of the upper. It is important that the water carried in the stream does not significantly overflow the lower pool when the pump is turned off. To prevent excessive overflow, either make the lower pool large enough to hold the stream's full volume of water or create a series of smaller pools along the stream's length that together hold all the water.

If the water flow seems to slow too much toward the middle of the stream, use another small pump to generate more current. Place the pump where it can most easily be hidden and run an outflow tube up to near where the still water begins. Camouflage both the pump and the tubing with stones. Keep the tube underwater and point it upward and into the middle of the stream. If you do this where the stream narrows, the increased current there will seem natural. Once the stream has been constructed and is fully functional, it can be planted (see chapter 5).

Placing the large boulders for the waterfall using a custom-designed and custom-built machine.

7

Bog Gardens

A Tiny Bog with Frogs and Bugs

Site condition

A bog garden is rarely considered an option for a really small property, especially when what is also desired is a water garden that can sustain flora and fauna. In this example, however, we find how both can be incorporated. There was little space within this garden environment to accommodate a water garden, a bog garden, and a living area, but for a household of two who wanted a plethora of living things around them, from fish, frogs, and snails to a variety of interesting water plants and some plants that grow only in a bog, it was just enough.

Site design

To maintain a living area large enough for a small table and a few chairs, the water feature had to be placed in a corner. The sun's path dictated the far left corner, which would also save the feature from becoming the depository of foliage and spent flowers from the thriving climbing hydrangea on the right. Here, in the corner, the water feature could be enjoyed from all areas of the garden without being in the way.

A rectilinear layout for this garden was certainly an option and would have worked well, especially given the retaining bench across the rear of the garden, which the owners wanted to keep. However, both owners lived and worked in a city and were in need of, as is so often the case, a reprieve from straight lines and hard angles. They wanted a more natural garden in an easy, free-flow design.

In keeping with the owners' wishes, the patio was given an undulant line and was made of irregularly shaped pieces of stone. Moss was later lovingly planted between the stone, which further added to the naturalness. The patio was made just large enough for it to be used (the garden seats six reasonably comfortably, if a little intimately), and as many planting areas as could be managed were created in irregular fashion along the garden's sides.

Water feature design

In keeping with the free-form style of the garden, the water and bog garden were likewise made as irregular as possible within the constraints of a very

BEFORE:

A genuine postage-stamp garden that was nevertheless large enough for a small patio, a small pond, and a tiny bog garden.

THE ENLARGING EFFECT OF WATER

Sometimes there is a tendency to think that a small space is too small for a water feature, that too much space is lost that could otherwise be planted or used for a table or chairs. In effect, water gardens add space by adding interest. Any element that draws the attention of any of our senses both expands and prolongs our experience of the garden, thereby enlarging it for us. Water features are excellent for this purpose. The delightful sound of cascading water, the reflections on a placid pool, the color and motion of swimming fish, the day- and night-blooming water lilies—few other elements offer so much in so little space. A bog can, contrary to what some might think, support as many plants as the same area of soil. In addition, bogs and water gardens permit the cultivation of exotic species that cannot be grown in garden soil.

An irregular pool and bog are fed by a waterfall with planting pockets to support ferns and other plants.

THE VIRTUE OF CORNERS

In homes and in gardens, corners often go unused. Since we don't want to put ourselves into a corner, corners make excellent locations for placing elements of interest. Locating a water garden in a corner of the property puts that space to maximum use. In a very small space, the corner becomes a focal point from everywhere in the garden, and we don't need to enter the corner to enjoy the myriad pleasures of a water feature.

limited space. The small waterfall, which was placed at the far end for maximum exposure, flows gently down a series of rocks and falls several inches into the pool. During the waterfall's construction, planting pockets were built in to accommodate ferns and other trailing plants that softened the stonework.

Patio stones come all the way up to the right side of the water garden, following the pool's irregular edge. On the left side the liner extends to the wood fence, but an additional wall was built inside the pond to retain soil. Small holes were left in the wall, allowing water to seep into an area that, once filled with soil, became the bog garden. This bog area remains moist, providing the perfect habitat for bog plants, which are those that cannot be grown in water but that need constantly moist soil.

An additional wall containing holes was built in the left side of the pond to create the bog area.

Planting

The original planting consisted primarily of an *Acer palmatum*, various hostas, the climbing hydrangea, and an eclectic mix of perennials. There was also a redvein enkianthus (*Enkianthus campanulatus*), and a dwarf spruce (*Picea pungens* 'Montgomery'). To these were added numerous bog and water-garden plants such as water mints (*Mentha aquatica*), water canna (*Canna* hybrid), water iris, water lilies, and giant arrowheads (*Sagittaria montevidensis*). See chapter 10.

An unpromising site was transformed into an intimate patio garden with a pond and bog garden. The layout was made free-form and informal, inducing a sense of the natural, and the water feature was designed accordingly within the constraints of a very narrow area. The result is a densely planted garden, inviting to people and wildlife alike.

A plethora of bog and water plants was added to the landscape.

A Garden in a Bog

A natural wetlands transformed into a diversely planted bog garden. Photo by John Glover.

Site condition

This was a natural bog, an area in which the ground is always moist or wet. Such an area can be made usable or attractive through two different approaches. The first is to drain away the water, prevent more water from flowing into the area, and replace the soil; in short, one gets rid of the bog. This method is costly and often not even possible if, for instance, the water comes from below. The second method is to enhance the area with attractive plants that thrive in boggy conditions. This latter approach was taken here.

Site design or water feature design

As a naturally existing boggy area, the site required no designing apart from selection and placement of plant species.

Planting

The bold foliage of skunk cabbage (*Lysichiton*) in the foreground and rhubarb (*Rheum*) in the background contain, between them, the finer textures of ferns, irises, and lamiastrums. Attractive through the season, this grouping is especially striking when the irises and lysichitons are blooming.

A naturally boggy area was transformed into an attractive garden of native wetland plants. All that was required was the planting of appropriate bog plants.

A Stream with Boggy Bank

Site condition

A natural stream creates a natural bog area along its banks. The shallowness of the stream permits the cultivation of bog plants that must have water over their roots as well as those that prefer the moist soil of a stream bank.

A stream with boggy banks provides the perfect habitat for diverse flora. Photo by John Glover.

THE LAW OF MANY AND THE EXCEPTION OF THE SINGULAR

It seems to be a law throughout nature that most things occur in groups and that singularity is the exception. A particular species of plant growing in a mass tends to thin at its margins and become interspersed with another species that, in turn, is also thin at the margins and dense at its center. Somewhere between these two merging groupings of plants there may be a third species or genus appearing singularly or in low numbers.

If space permits, a group can be repeated to enhance the sense of unity. It can also be allowed to drift into a third plant type at another location. Of course, this general model has countless variations, yet something of this sort is commonly found in nature and makes one of the most pleasing arrangements in a garden.

Site design or water feature design

As with the project on a garden in a bog, this site and situation were already in place, with the stream meandering slowly between boggy banks. All that was needed to render this an idyllic scene was sensitive and appropriate planting.

Planting

When creating a naturalistic planting, you should keep in mind how important it is to do as nature does. Groups of plants should be created that will drift into other groupings, an occasional singular specimen being planted here and there as an effective contrast. The arrangement of plant groups containing a single specimen of another species within it or nearby is among the more pleasing designs of nature and is often seen in fields or on hillsides.

Ferns, irises, skunk cabbages, lamiastrums, rhubarb, primulas, irises, and water forget-me-nots (*Myosotis scorpioides*) are distributed throughout this planting but they are in distinct groupings, with one plant type casually drifting into another. This is how nature works, and it makes for a thoroughly satisfying arrangement, since an arrangement that mimics nature is particularly satisfying in a setting where the stream is a natural one.

A natural stream was elevated above the ordinary by the simple but sensitive approach of creating drifts of naturalizing bog plants. A variety of floral and foliar harmonies and contrasts enrich the scene while the stones in the stream add a satisfying structural component.

YOU WILL NEED: *a liner, hole punch, landscape fabric, and gravel. Sphagnum moss and sand are optional.*

Bogs can be the easiest water feature to create or quite complicated, depending primarily on what plants you decide to grow. The more complex bogs usually occupy larger areas and are meant to simulate a natural bog as it might appear in the woods. The details of those creations I leave to other authorities; I instead treat the small, simpler garden bogs.

In the case of a stand-alone bog that is not connected to a pond, all you have to do is place a water-retentive liner in the ground to a couple of feet deep at the deepest places, bringing it up to grade at the sides. Small holes punctured through the liner and covered with small pea gravel or washed stone will create slow drainage and prevent the soil from souring. (You can also use landscape fabric instead of gravel or lay it beneath the gravel.) This material allows moisture to pass through while retaining the soil. The number of holes needed depends in part on the soil to be used. Heavy soil holds moisture longer, meaning that there should be more holes in the liner, whereas thin or sandy soil drains readily, in which case fewer holes are needed. Instead of filling the area underlain with liner with water, fill it with soil and plants before watering it.

To increase the range of plants to be grown, fill part of the planting area with a whole-fiber sphagnum moss and sand mix rather than soil. (Sphagnum moss naturally occurs in bogs and is the medium many bog plants normally grow in.) Doing this will help generate the proper pH some bog plants require. For other plants, you could also create some areas of higher elevation that will not remain as wet. However, if you intend to plant only standard margin or bog plants obtainable from water-garden supply houses, you will not need to use sphagnum moss or build higher elevations.

If the bog is built as part of a pond, simply extend the liner of the pond and build a permeable wall on the inside of the pond to separate the pond from the bog. A permeable barrier allows moisture to pass into the bog but keeps the soil out of the pond.

For regular, automatic wetting, a simple garden or soaker hose on a battery-powered timer will do. Alternatively, an irrigation line can be run to the bog that is powered by an electric, automatic timer set to water on specified days and times. One of these systems is recommended if regular hand watering will not be possible.

As a bog allows the cultivation of a wide range of plants that otherwise could not be grown, you should place the bog garden where these plants will provide maximum enjoyment. If the bog is part of a water garden, place it either at the back of the garden so that the plants can be seen across the pool or in such a way that the plants would occupy only part of the front of the garden so as not to obscure the pond. If the bog is a stand-alone feature, place it where it gets maximum visual exposure and the most sun with a little midday shade to reduce evaporation.

8

Tub Gardens

The Typical Tub

A tub garden created in a half whisky barrel, the perfect feature for displaying those plants that don't grow easily elsewhere. Photo by John Glover.

IF IT HOLDS WATER

If a container holds water—or if it can be made to—it qualifies as a candidate for the tub garden. Size hardly matters. Tin cans, watering cans, old basins, concrete vessels, hollowed stones, favorite old bowls—the possibilities are endless. Most vessels of most materials can be made watertight, so if it is attractive and not otherwise employed, consider it for the tub garden.

Location

Any old place where you've got space is the typical home for the typical tub. Its attraction to gardeners is its ability to display a clear pool of water supporting beautiful and unusual plants. Tub gardens do not need moving water to keep the water fresh, so you don't need a pump. An appropriate balance of aquatic life will provide that service. Just be sure to include a fish or two if you don't want mosquitoes; even one fish will guarantee zero mosquitoes.

Tub style

The typical tub garden is the half whisky barrel or wine barrel that is given water-retention capability through a sealant or rubber liner. It can be freestanding or sunk in the ground, and because of its previous contents, it resists decay quite admirably.

Site enhancement

The only site enhancement necessary with this tub garden is in the addition of the adjacent soil-planted pot containing a variegated yucca. The harmony this plant creates with the variegated water iris is all the adornment needed. It is a simple setting yet completely effective.

Planting

Iris laevigata 'Versicolor' is the vertical accent in the tub, while a water pennywort (*Hydrocotyle verticillata*) lines and softens the edges. A dwarf water lily is about to poke up through the water's surface.

A simple tub simply placed and planted makes a superb accent in the garden, adding interest and originality without overpowering the site.

Man Bathing in a Tub

Location

Tubs can go beautifully in a gardened setting, on a patio, by a front or back door—virtually anywhere there is light and about three square feet of space for the tub to sit on. There are many suitable locations for a tub garden: along a passageway where it will be seen only in coming and going, as a focal point for a patio, or as an integral and contrasting element within a garden bed. Here we focus on a tub garden within a garden.

Tub style

This tub is very cleverly designed, creating a completely captivating impact on the viewer. Although essentially the same mechanically as most tub gardens, it features a sculpted mask and hands, a secondary tub, and a secondary fountain. The pump is in the lower tub, recirculating the water to the frog on the edge of that tub and through a hole at the bottom to the top tub. The tubs themselves are ordinary whisky-barrel types.

Site enhancement

Decorative elements such as the rabbit and the river stones are placed around the tub to give it an established, finished look. Plants enclose the tub, creating a definite sense of place for it.

Planting

Grasses, Eastern hemlock, and creeping juniper enclose the tub garden. Inside the upper tub, common duck weed (*Lemna minor*) floats on the surface.

A cleverly and humorously designed tub in two parts brings considerable interest and liveliness to this portion of the garden. A whimsical, original element such as this tub removes us from our day-to-day concerns, helping us to relax and enjoy the garden and this little watery world of a tub garden.

A man bathing in a tub filled with common duckweed (*Lemna minor*), a frog and rabbit looking on. Photo by John Glover.

A Sunken Tub in a Flowery Corner

A sunken tub ornaments a planted corner. Notice that it is raised enough so as not to be a trip hazard. Photo by John Glover.

Location

There was certainly more room for in-ground planting in this corner, which is what would have been done normally. But see what a pleasant textural contrast and a difference of elements a sunken tub in this flowery corner makes.

Tub style

The tub is an ordinary wooden whisky barrel placed in a corner garden. Three quarters of it is below grade but enough extends above grade to reduce the amount of soil spilling in and to keep it from being a trip hazard.

Site enhancement

In this case, it is the tub that is enhancing an existing planted corner. The tub has a bright backdrop of variegated ornamentals and flowering peonies and shrubs. The tub itself is planted in delicate floating aquatics and boldly vertical black-leaved plants. It is set in a bed of sand, which provides a clean, uniform setting. Nearby are a group of river stones and another planting of black-leaved plants, helping to unite the tub with the surrounding garden.

Planting

Rhododendrons, mountain laurel (*Kalmia latifolia*), aucubas, and andromeda (*Pieris japonica*) provide the primary structural mass plantings. Here they are mixed with ferns, *Euonymus fortunei*, variegated irises, hostas, and a few scattered companions, which fill in the foreground.

An otherwise ordinary, planted corner is given considerable charm and interest by the placement of a tub that is almost completely buried in the ground. The element of water makes a pleasant contrast to the surrounding terrain.

Yellow Lilies in a Blue Bowl

Location

This was a corner of a patio bordering on a wildflower planting. It needed some architectural element that would not obscure the view of the wildflowers and beyond. The earthiness of the brick patio meant that something ornate was called for.

Tub style

A tub garden is, after all, only a container that holds water and that is planted appropriately. It can be made of anything, from wood to porcelain. Here an ornamental ceramic bowl was turned into a water garden. It is able to hold water because it has been fired.

Site enhancement

River rocks always look good near water. Here they help to visually contain and anchor the planted tub.

Planting

The water lily is a plant of *Nymphaea odoratum* 'Minor'. The *N. tetragona* 'Helvola' is in bud, and *Lysimachia nummularia* is the plant creeping over the rocks in front of the bowl. Behind the water feature is common thyme. The smooth, glossy surface of the bowl is accentuated by the coarse texture of the thyme while the elegant lilies are reflected in the painting on the bowl.

Yellow water lilies in a blue bowl with beautiful, contrasting common thyme (*Thymus vulgaris*) in full flower behind it. Photo by John Glover.

A lovely porcelain tub brings a rich and striking contrast to the brick paving and planting beyond. The beautiful, painted porcelain bowl is a work of art in itself. Filled with water and planted, it becomes a living work of art, forever changing, and always a pleasure, enhancing the setting in which it is placed.

YOU WILL NEED: *a container, drill, pump, tubing, and, if the container is not waterproof, a liner.*

Kits that include the tub, liner, hose, plants, and animal life (some even contain a pump) can be purchased complete—all you have to do is add water. Alternatively, these various items can be bought separately to create a custom tub. Here I discuss the basic components of the typical tub garden with fountain.

A tub, properly planted with a variety of oxygenating plants and stocked with a snail and a fish or two, will maintain fresh water that is free of unwanted mosquitoes and algae. The pump is not necessary to keep the water fresh but is often used for its ornamental value. If the flow of water into the tub sufficiently disturbs the water, you will not need fish to keep the water in a healthy state.

Most tubs sold for use as a water garden require a liner. The tub may come already lined or liners for use in tubs can be bought separately. Many

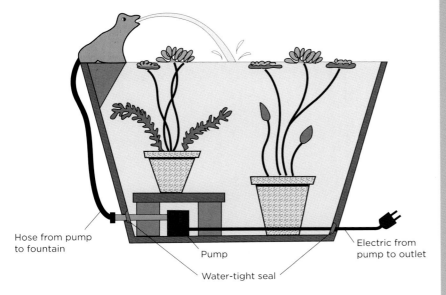

Hose from pump
to fountain

Pump

Water-tight seal

Electric from
pump to outlet

The typical tub garden with pump

old whisky and wine barrels are available, however, that are already water-tight, in which case all that is needed is a sealant to keep out toxins from the wood and insure water retention over time. Once a watertight condition is established, it is simply a matter of stocking the tub with appropriate flora and fauna for a functional, attractive tub garden. If, however, a pump is desired, you will have to do a little more work.

A small stream of water flowing into the tub from an ornamental foun-tain not only brings another dimension to the feature but it is also fairly eas-ily installed. To hide the water and electric lines, drill two holes into the tub for the water hose and the power cord from the pump. These holes should be only as large as necessary to take the tube and cord and the holes should be fitted with a watertight seal and siliconized on the inside and outside. Seals and silicones are available at plumbing supply houses. Run the tube to the fountain and the electric lines to an outlet and the job is done.

The tub should be set in place before it is filled and stocked. (If you put it on wheels, you can easily move it around) If it is to be buried in the ground, first fit it with a liner and pump (if you are using a pump), and then treat both the inside and the outside of the tub with a sealant to retard decay before you sink it. Once the tub is sunk, it can be planted and filled.

9

Natural Waterfalls

WATERFALLS, no matter the scale, are great. Not only do they look and sound wonderful (if they are well built), but the fish love them. One of the simple pleasures of life is watching fish sporting and thriving under a fall of water in a pond of any size. They will actually play under the falling water, clearly appreciating the richly oxygenated water.

In this chapter I focus specifically on waterfalls, some of which also appear in the chapters on pools and streams. The reason I specifically address waterfalls is because a reasonably well designed pool will, more often than not, possess a really badly designed waterfall. They're easy to get wrong and difficult to get right, at least aesthetically. However, there are principles behind creating a waterfall that looks right, and we will examine design elements that pertain to their creation by looking at a few well-designed and not so well-designed examples. It is useful to see what does not work so as to know what to avoid. We will also look at actual construction techniques.

The four common mistakes in the creation of waterfalls are selecting the wrong type of stone, placing both waterfall and surrounding stone poorly, making too small or too large a fall for the pool it feeds, and supplying too much or too little water for the size of the fall.

The most common of these mistakes is using the wrong stone. Streams in nature flow over stones that have been beneath the incessant influence of moving water for a very long time. These stones, known as river rock, river flats, or river rounds, are smooth and worn, and although they are commonly available, they are not easy to work with. Water that passes over a stone with a rounded edge tends to cling to the rock, follow the curve around to its underside, and then go under the rock; it tends not to cascade from the rock's edge.

The difficulties in working with river rock explain why so many waterfalls are built of rough granite recently taken from the interior of some mountainside and never before visited by so much as a raindrop. With their sharply angled edges, these stones control the flow and fall of water really well, but they often don't look right. It is possible to use massive pieces of stone that can bear a torrent of water; the drama of it all is captivating and convincing, provided the stones are reasonably well placed and the pool into which it spills is in scale.

In this example, except for the rock just above the main flow of water, these stones are well placed and the whole waterfall is quite convincing and satisfying. The rock at the top over which the water is flowing is not right for water flow as it is too rough. If not for the unfortunate angle of the rock above it, however, this very rough stone would seem perfectly fine. That

The massive scale of this fall is convincing, largely because of the skill-ful placement of the surrounding stones. Photo by John Glover.

badly laid rock, which in its off angle (meaning it is neither perpendicular nor parallel to the lay of the other stones or to the falls) breaks from the oth-erwise perfect horizontal and vertical arrangement of the other rocks and creates a disharmony that draws the eye. Were it level, all would appear perfect. We can see, too, that the pool into which the fall spills is of adequate size and that the surrounding stones are well chosen and well placed.

This small waterfall was built of stone not accustomed to water flowing over it. While the front area is convincing enough, the rear stone could have been better placed. Photo by John Glover.

This example has similar virtues and faults as the preceding one but on a smaller scale. None of the stone is appropriate for water flow, but the water does fall nicely. The water follows a meandering course and divides to fall from several points, all of which is quite pleasing. Additionally, the size of the fall is in scale with the pools and the volume of water is in scale with the fall. Better placement of the rear stones would have contributed to the overall effect, but on the whole, this waterfall is satisfying enough, particularly in the foreground.

The failings of this creation are in the rear stones over the first fall and in the surrounding stones. In waterfall construction, side or supporting stones are like supporting actors in a drama; they can either contribute to the overall effect or detract from it, depending on which are used and how they are placed. Here, the rear and side stones appear weak. They do not fit well together, which makes it appear a little unstable. A slight refitting of those stones to create a better sense of solidity would improve this otherwise attractive creation.

A tranquil pool is filled by water running from a tranquil fall. Everything about the garden in which this water feature has been created is sedate, mostly round, smooth, and peaceful.

This garden's waterfall is composed of smooth, water-washed stones, and even those above and to the sides of the fall are rounded. The water slides easily over the rock, making a gentle gurgling as it slips into the pool, contributing to the peaceful harmony that is the theme of the garden. The supporting stones of the waterfall are of correct type and shape, and they are well placed to contribute to the appearance of the falls. They fit closely against the waterfall and appear to have been worn by the water. The volume of flow is also suitable for this small water feature.

This entire garden is one of quiet repose characterized by soft, rounded curves.

A relaxed garden requires an undramatic waterfall and pool.

A natural pool in an informal setting.

This waterfall is similar to the immediately preceding one but has a little more action, a little more liveliness because the water falls a short distance into the pool. This feature could have been made even more dramatic—and to good effect—if water were falling from one stone to another and then into the pool. However, it works well as is. Both the size of the falls and the volume of water are in scale, and because it is a simple design, it fits the garden it is found in.

The natural fall is in keeping with the size of the pool but lively and attractive.

This waterfall is likewise in keeping with the pond and garden to which it belongs. In an intentionally junglelike setting, the falls look natural, if a little formless, as does the pool into which it flows. The fall is dramatic enough to cause a lively display, both visually and audibly, but it is still in proportion to the pool into which it flows.

Though impressive, this fall is much too dramatic for the pool into which it flows. Photo by John Glover.

An overly elaborate waterfall that makes use of the wrong kinds of stone. The side stones are poorly placed.

The waterfalls on this page reflect poor stone selection, poor placement, and in the case of the overly dramatic feature, a lack of scale. Both waterfalls are built of stone unaccustomed to the passage of water, and in both, the stones are in a jumble as though they have been haphazardly scattered about. In the above example, there is the additional flaw of a much too large waterfall for the pool into which it spills. It lacks scale.

Constructed as an artesian well, this pool and waterfall feed into a meandering stream in a small urban backyard.

Designed as an artesian well with water bubbling up between what appears to be a natural stone grouping, the water flows over a stone and into a stream. The size of the waterfall, which is on only one level, is in keeping with the stream it flows into. Though located in an urban backyard, this waterfall arrangement is quite convincing with all the stones relating well to one another. The stone over which the water flows is a perfect waterfall stone. It is smooth and curved with a downward sloping face. Water flows easily from it.

A delicate, multitiered waterfall in scale with a tiny pool and bog garden.

Possibly the most enjoyable waterfall is the multitiered, with water falling from stone to stone and finally into a pool. Such a feature can be employed in intimate settings if the principles of scale are allowed to govern. This small fall and pool with an adjoining bog is a case in point; the entire setting is minute, the pond and adjoining bog are tiny, and the waterfall is appropriately delicate.

A small natural pool with waterfall, where a torrent splashes into a small pool. Photo by Todd Davis.

Here we have a multitiered, torrential waterfall splashing into a small pool. At first this seems entirely captivating, and it is certainly quite lively and entertaining. But upon contemplation, we come to a curious observation: This tremendous activity is producing no effect. The stones over which the water rushes are not in the least worn and they show no signs of the wear of water that would naturally occur with the passage of time.

Well, new streams do happen. Watercourses get diverted or cut their way through new territory, find new stones, over which the water will pass, directing the stream's course. Though this particular feature might have been done differently, it is done well, making us believe this is a natural pool with a natural waterfall. The stones are certainly in scale with the flow of water, and the dimensions all work together. Although the pond is small, it gives the appearance of being deep enough to accommodate—and to have been created by—such a heavy flow of falling water.

YOU WILL NEED: *river stone of various sizes and liner material.*

A well-built waterfall is a thing of beauty, but as we have seen, "well-built" is the key term. Too many waterfalls in home gardens are sorry affairs for a variety of reasons, including incorrect stone being used, the waterfalls themselves being out of scale with the pools they flow into and with the amount of water flowing over them, and the rock in and around the waterfall being unnatural in appearance. There is the additional problem with getting the water to flow over and not under the stones, which I discuss further in this chapter. Unless proper technique is used, a waterfall, instead of being pleasing, can be quite unsatisfying. I will therefore focus on the techniques for achieving good aesthetics as well as on the practical considerations of making a waterfall work.

Preparing the area

Usually, you want water to flow from a fall into a pool with effects that are both audio and visual. This means there will be rocks above and below the apparent water source, and that water will flow over rocks, falling either some distance into the pool below or from rock to rock and then into the pool. As water passes over rocks, it also clings to their surfaces and, to some extent, runs under the underside of the rocks. To allow for water running under the rocks, the entire ground area around the waterfall should slope toward the pool and be covered in liner. Otherwise, any water that splashes out or runs under the bottoms of rocks will end up outside the pond and the pond will quickly drain. Similarly, if the rocks over which the water flows slope very slightly toward the pool, that slight angle will help ensure that water stays in the fall until it ends up in the pool instead of draining away unseen behind the fall. (I discuss this in greater detail in the section on placing stones.) The liner that is under the waterfall needn't be the same piece that lines the pond. A separate piece placed over the pond liner works just as well, as long as water cannot run under it.

Selecting the stones

We have all seen falls made from rocks freshly dug from deep within some mountain, complete with a jagged edge, posing as a natural spillway for either torrent or trickle. Such rocks are used because water falls well from them, but they are rarely convincing.

The stone from which water finally falls should be of a certain type and shape, and the best stones for waterfalls are river flats. They are already water worn so they naturally lend themselves to a waterfall, and most stone yards carry them. A good waterfall rock, however, will also have a slightly concave upper surface that slopes downward toward its front edge, a downward slanting face on an angle, and ideally, a slightly convex bottom surface near the front edge. Water looks right on this type of stone (not on just any river flat), and as it reaches the edge of the rock, it runs down the face a short distance and falls directly into the pool instead of clinging to the rock and flowing backward and beneath it, which water will do with any other rock shape, especially when the flow is light. A stone such as this is not easy to find but it does exist and is well worth the hunt. Many stone yards keep open bins of river flats and river rounds. If you pull through them a while, you should come up with some very satisfactory stones for your waterfall.

Placing the stones

The best suggestion for learning about stone placement is to look at some natural falls or well done man-made falls. Many botanic gardens have really excellent streams with falls, and spending a little time near these (or with photos) will help considerably. With a little sensitivity and patience, you too can achieve a very attractive creation. As you place the stones, stand back and take in the effect, stone by stone. Begin placing them from the bottom of the waterfall and work toward the top. As you work upward, each succeeding stone will rest on the one beneath, and the water will naturally flow from one to the other without getting behind the stones.

Although it is a good idea to slope the stones slightly toward the pool to ensure that the water travels forward and not away from the pond, a common mistake is to slope the rocks too much, which never looks right. When rocks are sloped too much, the fall seems to be tipping forward. The stones should appear to be level, and a series of apparently level stones stepping down, one beneath the other, the lower one protruding out further than the one above, is quite satisfying to see.

You will notice with natural streams that there are always stones to the sides of the waterfall that are not in the water but are a part of the arrangement. Often these are larger boulders and they help direct the course of the water flow. Be sure to include these larger stones in your creation as they add balance to and often help support the horizontal stones. In the little nooks that are created by the larger stones, set smaller rounded rocks of various sizes. These smaller rocks are always a part of a natural waterfall scene and will give a complete, finished look to the fall.

Size and flow

The size of the waterfall, no matter the amount of water flowing over it, should be in proportion to the size of the pond. A massive stone construction over a tiny pond will always be visually dissatisfying even if the water volume is proportional. The quantity of water flowing should be in proportion to the size of both the fall and the pond. In other words, a large construction of stones for the waterfall should have a considerable quantity of water flowing into a good-sized pond. It looks silly if a lot of water is flowing into a small pool or coming out of a small fall.

The reverse is not as true. A small construction over a large pond is not as inappropriate as a large construction over a small pond for the same reason that a small flow of water into a large pond is not inappropriate. In nature, ponds can form over a long time, and a small channel emerging from an embankment with a slight but consistent flow of water can easily create a fairly large pond. However, we must realize that in home constructions, this water is continuously recirculating, and in order for the water to be cleaned and aerated properly, the full volume of the pond must cycle through at least once every two hours. A small flow into a pond with a lot of water will not achieve this degree of circulation.

The size of the waterfall is simply a matter of how many and what size stones you use. The water volume is determined by the size of the pump, the distance and elevation the water is pumped, and the smallest diameter of hose through which the water flows. For example, a seven-hundred-and-fifty-gallon per hour pump can deliver a fairly impressive flow of water if it is not pumped too far or too high. A screw clamp on the outflow tube can cut that down to a trickle, should that be desired, without harming the pump. (Do not, however, attempt to restrict the intake capacity of the pump or you'll burn it out.) It is best, therefore, to buy more pump than you need as the output can always be decreased with a clamp or gate valve, but you will never get a five-hundred-gallon-per-hour pump to deliver more than five hundred gallons in an hour.

10

Flora

HERE WE WILL CONSIDER the planting and care of four categories of water features: the in-ground and raised, formal and informal pool; the tub garden; the bog garden; and the stream. For simplicity's sake, I will refer to any in-ground or raised water feature (other than a tub garden), whether formal or informal, simply as a pool.

Of all the types of water features, only the wall fountain does not get planted. Among the rest, the informal, formal, in-ground, and raised pools are all treated the same. These pools can be embellished by the same plants, planted in the same manner, and cared for in much the same way. The tub garden is slightly different in that greater care as to plant selection must be taken, especially if there is no recirculating pump, and fewer plant species are suitable. The bog garden stands alone as unsuitable for most of the aquatics available to the pool, though many margin plants used in pools are suitable for the bog garden. A stream may have plants both in the water and along the banks, and I likewise treat it separately.

PLANTS FOR THE POOL

Three categories of plants are necessary for a balanced ecosystem if the pool is to remain healthy, able to support animal life such as fish, and, when well combined with those plants, it is to create the most pleasing aspect. The plants in the first category are the deep-water aquatics such as water lilies and lotus plants. The roots, which are in soil in the water, must always be in water. Their mature leaves are above or on the water's surface. The second category contains the submerged plants that are rooted under water and that must live entirely below the surface of the water. Plants in the third category are the margin plants, which are those that grow at the water's edge in moist or wet soil, the foliage of which may be upright, floating, or creeping. Each of these plant categories (and various species among them) requires a particular planting depth, which I address in the discussion of each type. In addition to these are floating plants, which are plants with roots in the water and that float on the water's surface. These may or may not be included in your water garden; often they are not because of their tendency to propagate rapidly. However, they can be quite attractive, they perform the same functions as submerged plants (they use nitrogen, reducing algae growth), and their dangling water roots provide havens for small fish.

As with most aspects of water gardening, there are formulas for how much of what item to include based on the quantity of water. For example, the following table represents the proportions suggested by suppliers of pond flora and fauna, but as will be explained, this table is only a guide.

Though commonly promoted and published, the table has several problems, primarily because of the variables that affect all this. For example, if

The many floating leaves and blossoms of water lilies help keep algae growth down while beautifying the water garden. The tropical *Nymphaea* 'Albert Greenberg' flowers are a bright combination of red, yellow, and pink colors. Photo by Lilypons.

SURFACE AREA IN SQUARE FEET	TOTAL LENGTH OF ALL FISH	SUBMERGED	AQUATICS	FLOATING OR MARGINAL	SNAILS
4	4 inches	12 stems (2 bunches)	0	1	2
8	8 inches	24 stems (4 bunches)	0	1 to 2	4
12	12 inches	36 stems (6 bunches)	1	2	6
100	100 to 200 inches	600 stems (100 bunches)	5 to 10	18 to 33	50 to 100

there is strong circulation and accompanying filtration from a larger than necessary pump, considerably more fish can be sustained than the above table recommends. In addition, this table suggests that a tub garden cannot have a lily but of course no one intends that; a tub garden may have one or more lilies, as well as other plants. The table also only considers the pool's surface area, not its volume, which of course affects everything. A deeper pond will support more life, particularly if oxygenation is supplied through submersible plants or a bubbler. (A bubbler pumps air into the pond helping to oxygenate the water.)

Another factor in calculating the amount of life that a pool can sustain is filtration. The greater the degree of filtration, the more fish can be accommodated. Less filtration and more fish will result in cloudier water. To ensure clear water, you must have adequate filtration, increase the number of submersibles, reduce the number of fish, and allow only about 40 percent of the water to show. In general, 60 percent of the water's surface area should be shaded by lily pads or other floating plants, as this keeps algae growth down. In very large ponds, however, a smaller percentage of the water's surface needs be covered.

A five-foot by five-foot pond (twenty-five square feet in total) with good aeration and adequate filtration will easily accommodate—and be well provided with—two medium-sized water lilies, a few floating plants, a couple of margin plants, several to approximately eight bunches of submersibles, and several snails. In a pond this size, anywhere from four to fifteen small to medium fish will do well and look good. Although these numbers do not correspond exactly with the table, they do work, so use the table as a reliable guide, but as a guide only.

Deep water aquatics

WATER LILY (*Nymphaea*)
Hardiness zone of hardy types: Zones 3—11; tropical varieties can be grown in Zones 3—11, but overwinter in Zones 10 and 11 only.

The most common aquatic plants are the water lilies. There are hardy and tropical species, both of which can be used in colder climates such as the North Eastern United States but the tropical will survive only in Zone 11. In the colder climates, the tropicals will be grown as annuals and must be

Some lilies, such as the night-blooming tropical *Nymphaea* 'Red Flare', hold their blossoms above the water's surface. Photo by Lilypons.

The lavender-blue of *Nymphaea* 'Blue Star' is among the many shades of blue that water lilies offer. Photo by Lilypons.

replaced each year unless you choose to lift and clean the tubers and put them in distilled water in a jar that you store in a cool, dark place. Certain tropical water lilies are more shade tolerant than most hardies, which can be a reason for using them. Keep in mind, though, that the minimum amount of light for the most shade-tolerant hardy or tropical plant is three to four hours of direct sun.

Planting depth for water lilies depends on the species. The depth of water covering the soil ranges from six inches to more than two feet, with any given plant being able to thrive within a wide range. Twelve inches of water above the pot is common but not a rule. Water lilies are most often planted in pots placed on the bottom of the pond or on ledges, but if planting pockets have been built into the pond and filled with heavy soil or a sand and soil mix, they can be planted directly in the pockets, obviating any need for the sometimes unsightly containers. One attractive method of providing planting places for lilies and other aquatics or marginals is to build stone planters with river stone and mortar into the inside of the pond after the liner is in place.

There are said to be about seventy species and cultivars of water lilies that display an astonishing array of variations. Some are night blooming, some are fragrant, some hold their flowers above the pond surface while most flowers float on the surface. Doubles and singles show a variety of flower and petal forms, some have bloom times that vary as to when they bloom and for how long. Dwarf, medium, large, and giant species have leaves of various sizes, spread, and quantity, and flower colors range from pure white through pale to deep pink, red, yellow, peach, apricot, blue, purple, and lavender, with many changing their color as they mature or as the day progresses. In addition to the wonderful beauty of water lily blossoms, their leaves are also attractive. Leaves floating on the water's surface provide shade for fish, serve as launching (and lunching) pads for frogs, and keep down algae growth. Water lilies are surely a must for any pool that can sustain them.

Planting water lilies is not difficult. They thrive in heavy garden soil with ample clay that is not mixed with humus, manure, vermiculite, or any other lightweight soil amendment that tends to float out of the pot and sully the water's surface. They can be purchased as undeveloped rhizomes or, more commonly, as rhizomes with fully developed stalks, leaves, and even flower buds, though these first buds tend to drop off. You can plant lilies singly or in groups of two or three if the container is large enough.

Slender white petals and a yellow center make *Nymphaea* 'Charles Thomas' among the most elegant lilies. Photo by Lilypons.

Generally, tropical water-lily tubers are planted upright and placed in a pot with an eight- to ten-inch diameter per rhizome. Hardy water lilies grow more horizontally, so they need a wider pot to accommodate the length of the rhizome. A pot of around fourteen inches in diameter is recommended, and many say that a fabric pot is the most desirable. Place the rhizome in the pot in a depression of several inches of soil and cover with soil such that the crown's growing tip (which end contains the growing tip will be evident) is just above soil level. Press in fertilizer tabs (usually two per rhizome), firm the soil around the rhizome, cover with not more than an inch of gravel or small stones, and place the pot in the pond with six to eighteen inches of water above soil level. If the stalks are quite short or not yet grown and you want to be more precise with the water depth, place the container in less water and lower it further into the pond over the next few weeks as the leaf and flower stalks grow. Otherwise, a permanent depth of twelve to twenty-four inches above the soil is a good average.

Lilies like tranquil water so be sure to place them in relatively undisturbed water away from a waterfall or they will not thrive. As with any garden, leave enough room between pots to allow the plant's foliage sufficient room for development. The flowers and foliage of water lilies reproduce throughout the growing season, and both fertilization and removal of dead growth are part of the upkeep. Tools that make these tasks easy are available from aquatic plant purveyors to aid in both these procedures.

Yellow stamens, a deep-hued center, and lighter outer petals are characteristics of many water lilies, including this *Nymphaea* 'Rosy Morn', which gives them a kind of glow. Photo by Lilypons.

LOTUS (*Nelumbo*)

Hardiness zones 4—11, except the Pacific Northwest and Alaska, where they should not be grown.

It is curious that the lotus is not more widely grown considering its ease of cultivation, the extraordinary foliage, the exceptional beauty and lovely fragrance of the flower, the legendary seed pod (it is of considerable value in dry arrangements), and the fact that it doesn't even need a pond to grow in. Yet for every thousand ponds that contain a water lily, it seems that only one will have a lotus. Possibly its price—over twenty-five dollars in some cases—limits its popularity, but few plants give more for that price. Indeed, few plants give as much no matter the price.

Several varieties of lotuses are commonly available including grandifloras, which produce exceptionally large blossoms that are held five to seven feet above the water, and miniatures, which produce a smaller flower held two to five feet above the water. Naturally, the miniatures require a smaller pot and less space.

All lotuses are easy to plant. A thirty-quart pot is recommended for most of them but give the miniature varieties a two- to three-gallon pot. The standards require a pot with a large diameter that is at least eighteen inches across and deep enough to allow for two inches of soil over the tuber and two to four inches of water over the soil. Make sure the pot is made of hard rubber or plastic, and do not plant the lotus directly into the pond as the intensely vigorous roots can penetrate an EPDM of sixty mil as well as other

Among the most tranquil scenes in life is that of a water lily floating on a pond. Here *Nymphaea* 'Texas Dawn' brings light to the early morning. Photo by Lilypons.

Nelumbo 'Charles Thomas' has pink to purple petals with maroon-stained tips. The foliage reaches two to five feet above the water. Photo by Lilypons.

liner materials, creating leaks and allowing them to establish themselves elsewhere. For the same reason, the pots should not have a hole in the bottom. These plants can be very invasive and even impossible to control.

Fill the pot three quarters full with the same heavy soil you would use for the lily and place the tuber in it with the smaller, growing-tip end pointed upward. Cover the tuber with two inches of soil and half to one inch of small gravel (smooth, rounded river gravel looks best). Be careful of the growing tip, which you should leave exposed. Lotuses are highly productive plants and profit from regular fertilizing, but too much fertilizer will contribute to vegetative growth at the expense of the flowers. How much fertilizer to give will depend on the type used, so read the individual fertilizer instructions carefully. Place the pot where it will get a minimum of five hours of direct sun, which need not be in the pond. As long as water is kept in the pot, the lotus can be placed at the pond edge or, indeed, anywhere in the garden, though keeping it sunk in the ground is best. A Mosquito Dunk (a bioinsecticide in solid form that is placed in water) will control mosquitoes, though fish will do the job too if a large enough container is used to plant the lotuses in.

Use similar planting procedures for other deep-water plants such as variegated water clovers (*Marsilea mutica* 'Variegata'), water hawthorn (*Aponogeton distachyos*), and yellow floating heart (*Nymphoides peltata*).

A tulip lotus, *Nelumbo nucifera* 'Shirokunshi' opens as a sun within a sun within a sun. It reaches two to five feet above the water's surface. Photo by Lilypons.

SUBMERSIBLES

Submersibles, which are visible when you peer beneath the water's surface, are graceful, attractive additions to the water garden. They provide grazing and oxygen for fish and hiding places for fry, and they are especially valuable for absorbing nutrients that would otherwise go to feeding algae, which in turn helps keep the water clear. Many are a favorite food for fish so should be covered with a net through which they can grow without being destroyed. Since these plants absorb their nutrients from the water, they need only be planted for anchorage. They are best placed in clean sand with a light covering of pebbles. Usually sold in bunches, submersible plants can be planted at any depth below water that receives sufficient light, but they are best seen just beneath the surface, where they thrive (any portions of the plant left exposed to air will die). None should be planted in the wild or remain uncontained; several states have prohibited some submersibles. I provide brief descriptions of several excellent species that are commonly available.

CABOMBA CAROLINIANA

Zones 6–11

Washington grass, perhaps most often associated with aquariums, has delicate, fernlike, fan-shaped foliage. It is very effective when planted in clumps, soon becoming a favorite haunt of fish. Give this plant full sun.

ELODEA CANADENSIS

Zones 5–11

Canadian pondweed is a somewhat coarse yet attractive grassy plant with threadlike branches covered in small, lancelike leaves. Also called anacharis, this is another excellent filter plant that helps keep the water clean and it is a favorite food for fish.

CERATOPHYLLUM DEMERSUM

Zones 5–11

Hornwort is more tolerant of shade than most submersibles and can be planted deeper, up to two feet below the water's surface. This is another fish favorite for its oxygenating capacity and as a refuge for small fry. It presents a delicate appearance with whorls of filamentary leaves spaced along a slender stalk.

MYRIOPHYLLUM SPECIES

Zones 4–11

Milfoil is another delicate looking plant and excellent filter. The long, filament-like leaves surrounding stems up to three feet long draw nutrients from the water, helping to keep down algae. This plant provides fish with a refuge as well as plenty of oxygen.

Nelumbo 'Tai Zhen' is a miniature lotus that grows one to three feet tall. It can be planted in a pond or a pot on land as long as the pot holds a couple of inches of water or a pond. Photo by Lilypons.

MARGIN OR SHALLOW-WATER PLANTS

"Margin" and "shallow" are terms applied to plants that can grow in soil in shallow water or in soil that simply remains wet but has no visible water. They might also be called bog plants; in fact, many are found in the bog, but as bog planting is treated separately, I will confine this discussion to the planting of pots placed in the pond. The list of margin or shallow-water plants includes many irises, a wide variety of broad-leaved plants, floating leaved plants, creeping plants, rushes, reeds, and grasses.

Margin plants are wonderful for integrating an in-ground pond with the surrounding landscape or for simply dressing up a raised formal or informal pool. Sun and shade varieties, hardies, and tropicals grow to heights of several inches or seven feet. They can be grown singly, massed in borders, or interwoven, one species with another for textural and color harmonies

Canadian pondweed (*Elodea canadensis*) is an excellent natural filter and offers a good hideout for small fry. Photo by Lilypons.

and contrasts. Here I address the planting of several of the more popular margin plants.

IRISES

Zones 4–11; some in zones 6–11

Irises can be planted as bare-root rhizomes with foliage or without. Use heavy garden soil in a one-gallon container or place two or more rhizomes in a larger container with the growing tips pointing upward. Cover the rhizomes with two to three inches of soil. Add fertilizer tabs, cover with a half to one inch of small stone, and place the container at the pond edge with up to four inches of water over the soil. If the container is placed above the water line, be sure it has a hole in the bottom, as the soil must remain wet. To hide the container, plant the pond's edges with floating margin plants (see the section on floating margin plants below). Commonly available and popular species are yellow flags, *Iris versicolor*, and the Louisiana Hybrids, all of which have many cultivars. All these irises are available in a range of growing heights and in colors from white through yellow, lavender, blues, and purples.

Iris ×*fulvala* 'Pledge'. Clumps of iris will naturalize as margin plants in the pond or bog garden. Photo by Lilypons.

Broad-leaved margin plants

SAGITTARIA SPECIES

Zones 5–11

Among the most popular of the margin plants is arrowhead, a Native American plant that grows to twenty-four inches. It needs heavy soil placed from zero to twelve inches below water in sun or part shade. If underwater, it will produce juvenile, grasslike foliage that helps oxygenate the water. As the plant matures—or as water levels drop—the distinctive arrowhead-shaped leaves appear, followed in spring to fall by very pretty stalks of pure white blossoms with yellow centers. Arrowheads are an excellent addition to the pond margin and should be placed in the foreground where the lovely blossoms may be most thoroughly enjoyed. Popular species are *Sagittaria latifolia*, which needs zero to six inches of water and blooms through the summer, and *S. australis* 'Benni' with burgundy foliage.

The beautiful blossoms of *Sagittaria latifolia* last through the summer. Photo by Lilypons.

THALIA DEALBATA

Zones 6–11

Not for the small pond, thalias thrive in full sun or a little shade, with the top of the soil under zero to twelve inches of water. At maturity they can shoot up to six feet in clumps as wide, but if kept in smaller containers, their size will be less. The blue-green foliage is spear shaped on long stalks. In late spring to early fall, blossoms appear in clusters of purple flowers at the end of stems that rise well above the foliage. They create a dramatic effect in the medium to large pool.

PONTEDERIA CORDATA
Zones 3—11

Pickerel rush is another North American native that colonizes easily in full or part sun and can be propagated by division or seed. It stands thirty inches tall with spear-shaped foliage and needs zero to twelve inches of water over the soil. The stalks of violet-blue flowers, which are useful in bouquets, appear from spring into fall. A white variety is less commonly available. Pickerel rush is an excellent margin plant for the medium to large pool.

Floating margin plants

MARSILEA MUTICA
Zones 6—11

This water clover is a beautiful plant with floating foliage. Plant in moist soil or in several inches of water, but be aware that this is a very aggressive plant that should be contained. The two-tone glossy green foliage makes lovely patterns on the water's surface, particularly when fully surrounded by water, so it is worth the trouble of using a concrete block or other necessary support to get the plant in the middle of the pool. Alternatively, place the pot at the pond's edge and enjoy this flowerless margin plant from there.

NYMPHOIDES PELTATA
Zones 6—11

Yellow floating heart or water fringe (so-called because of the fringed blossom) is another of those margin plants that must be contained or it will take up all the available space. The attractive, heart-shaped foliage is glossy green and sometimes maroon. It is somewhat reminiscent of a water lily but smaller and far more productive. The distinctive yellow blossoms stand several inches above the floating foliage throughout the summer in either full sun or part shade. Pots should be beneath three to twelve inches of water. *Nymphoides cristatum* produces a very pretty white flower with a yellow center and is hardy in Zones 8—11.

LUDWIGIA SEDIOIDES
Zones 9—10

Mosaic plant is probably the most elegant of the floating leaved plants. Its red and bright green, diamond-shaped leaves in whirling rosettes give it a galactic look, as though it were its own world of spinning constellations. Although it must be grown as an annual in zones colder than 9, the patterns

At six feet tall, *Thalia dealbata* makes a strong accent in the rear of a medium or large pond. Photo by Lilypons.

Pickerel rush (*Pontederia cordata*) colonizes easily in full or part sun. Photo by Lilypons.

Parrot feather (*Myriophyllum aquaticum*) is a superb edging for the pond margin and provides good spawning grounds and a safety habitat for young fry. Photo by Lilypons.

Rainbow plant (*Houttuynia cordata*) makes an excellent edging or margin plant. Photo by Lilypons.

it adds to the water garden are worth the seasonal repotting. Place the one-gallon container in a sunny spot one to two feet below the water's surface. You can control its growth by cutting it back, and if you place the cuttings in water, they can be repotted when rooted.

Creeping margin plants

HYDROCOTYLE VERTICILLATA
Zones 5–11

Water pennywort is traditionally grown in soil. However, it is said to be a true "floater" in that it does not need contact with the soil but can be grown above water, the leaves clambering along the pond edge, floating on the water's surface, or remaining completely submerged. It is grown for its round, glossy, attractive foliage and is best appreciated in the foreground of the pool. Planted as a margin plant in a container, it does best with three to twelve inches of water over the soils's surface.

MYRIOPHYLLUM AQUATICUM
Zones 6–11

Parrot feather is a distinctive foliar plant with feathery blue-green leaves that will climb along the pond edge or form floating masses in the pool. Grown trailing in the water along the edges, parrot feather makes good spawning grounds. It prefers full sun or part but not dense shade. Place the planted pots in one to twelve inches of water, and in cold climates, lower them to well below ice level for winter storage.

MENTHA AQUATICA
Zones 6–11

Watermint, planted in wet soil or in containers with zero to two inches of water over the top, is a superb margin plant for softening the edge of a pond. When planted directly in soil, however, regular pruning and thinning will be necessary, as watermint is a vigorous and invasive creeper. The aromatic foliage is one of its positive attributes, as are the purple flowers borne above the masses of crinkly leaves in sun or light shade.

HOUTTUYNIA CORDATA
Zones 6–11

Rainbow plant is among those ornamental perennials that grows nearly anywhere, from dry to wet and rich to poor soil. It can be invasive if given too rich a soil. As a water-garden plant, it makes a brilliant edging with heart-shaped leaves streaked with red to maroon as well as white and several shades of green. Plant *Houttuynia cordata* in heavy soil in a quart container (or larger) in as much as twelve inches of water.

Grasses, reeds, and rushes

ACORUS CALAMUS

Zones 4–11

Sweet flag, so called for its citrusy fragrant foliage, is among the best vertical accents, even for a small pond, with iris-like leaves that are from two to four feet tall depending on the variety. *Acorus calamus* 'Variegatus' is a brightly variegated cultivar reaching to about thirty inches, its cream and yellow stripes making a striking contrast with broad-leaved margin plants such as *Thalia dealbata*. Plant in containers with up to six inches of water over the top. Dwarf variegated sweet flag, *A. gramineus* 'Variegatus', a petite version of the above, grows to twelve inches and needs zero to four inches of water.

A variegated foliage of this cat tail brings a bright accent to the pond. Photo by Lilypons.

TYPHA

Zones 2–11

Several species of cat tails ranging from eighteen inches to seven feet tall all bear the showy catkins characteristic of summer wetlands, marshes, and swamps. *Typha angustifolia* and *T. latifolia* are both Native American plants that grow to seven feet, and both need wet soil and up to twelve inches of water over the top of the container. *Typha angustifolia* has narrower leaves growing up to four feet, the flower spike rising above the leaves. The graceful cat tail *T. laxmannii* is a more delicate species to forty-eight inches tall, and *T. minima* is a dwarf variety that is excellent in the small pond as it reaches only a foot and a half. Place the taller varieties toward the rear of the pool as a backdrop. All cat tails should be grown in containers as they are invasive in soil.

ELEOCHARIS TUBERCULOSA

Zones 1–4.

Chinese water chestnut is a rush growing to three feet tall in moist soil or in up to twelve inches of water. The leaf is a tubelike, jointed stem at the end of which flower spiklets are produced in summer. *Eleocharis montevidensis* (sand spike-rush) is a delicate, twelve-inch rush that needs to be covered in up to two inches of water. It makes an excellent accent for a small pool or an edging for larger pools. *Eleocharis quadrangulata* reaches twenty-four inches in zero to six inches of water. The leaves are squared, hence the common name square-stem spike-rush.

Cat tail (*Typha latifolia*), a Native American species, reaches seven feet tall in zero to twelve inches of water. Photo by Lilypons.

Chinese water chestnut (*Eleocharis dulcis*) is one of the several rushes that provides vertical accents in the water garden. Photo by Lilypons.

DULICHIUM ARUNDINACEUM

Zones 6—11

Dwarf bamboo is a Native American plant reaching eighteen inches in full to part sun. Though not overly aggressive, it is best grown in a container with zero to four inches of water over the top. The delicate, feathery foliage makes an excellent edging or accent plant for small pools and tub gardens.

FLOATING PLANTS

Floating plants are those considered to be true floaters. Planting them is a matter of tossing them into the pool and letting them blow where they will. Their roots help cleanse the water by drawing off nutrients that would otherwise feed green water algae. Many of them are extraordinarily prolific and need to be culled from the pool lest they cast too much shade on the plants beneath and inhibit the oxygenation of the water from the air. Add the excess plants to the mulch pile.

EICHHORNIA CRASSIPES

Zones 10—11

Water hyacinth is another tender plant wanting warmth and light. Although the name and physical description—glossy, rounded leaves growing in an upward-turned rosette with pale lavender blossoms through the summer—sound exceedingly attractive, the plant is, in fact, somewhat coarse when not in bloom. It will not bloom unless it receives ample sun. Water hyacinth often does not look good in formal ponds or in very small ponds as it has considerable bulk, in part because of the rapidly increasing progeny that it sends out in all directions, which can look messy.

PISTIA STRATIOTES

Zones 10—11

Water lettuce, which actually looks more like a miniature cabbage with velvety green, fluted leaves, is a tropical floater. It prefers full to nearly full sun and still, shallow water but grows in deeper water as well. In ideal conditions, water lettuce grows so profusely that it will likely add considerably to your mulch bin.

Dwarf bamboo (*Dulichium arundinaceum*) is among the best vertical accents for the small pool. Photo by Lilypons.

PLANTING THE STREAM

The difficulty with planting a man-made stream arises from the fact that the soil just outside the stream, which would be boggy in a natural setting and therefore able to support many of the margin plants so far discussed, is not. Unless planting pockets are built inside the stream, there is not much place for water plants to naturalize. These difficulties can nevertheless be overcome, and suitable planting arrangements can be created, giving even the liner-built stream a completely natural look.

For example, several species of iris occur in boggy ground along the banks of streams, and though those kinds won't survive in the dry soil outside the man-made stream, other iris species will—and they will look right along its banks. Various grasses, their graceful leaves and catkins nodding over the stream, can also contribute enormously to the natural appearance of the stream garden. Ferns growing right up to the stream edge are also suitable and, given ample shade, so are hostas, astilbes, and aquilegias. Leucothoe plants look good too, as do violets and a dwarf weeping hemlock or two. Between and among the rocks in the stream and along the stream's edge, sweet woodruff (*Galium odoratum*) is a superb creeping cover that needs only the tiniest pockets of soil. Once started, sweet woodruffs will spread to any available niche. Place violets and dicentras a little higher up the banks, and on the rocks themselves grow mosses.

Larger shrubs suitable along a stream's edge are berberis, *Hydrangea macrophylla* and *H. quercifolia*, *Cornus alba* or *C. sericea*, *Kerria japonica*, and *Vaccinium angustifolium*. A bit further away from the stream itself, a weeping cherry (*Prunus subhirtella* 'Snow Fountains') is superb when seen near a stream.

PLANTING THE BOG GARDEN

Any of the margin plants I have discussed in this chapter that can stand in zero inches of water (meaning that although they only need wet soil they can also be immersed in water) are suitable for the bog. The following perennials and shrubs are additional plants that take boggy conditions.

ANDROMEDA POLIFOLIA
Zones 2–8; Zones 9–11 if humid

This plant is called bog rosemary because it resembles *Rosmarinus* and grows in sphagnum bogs. The overall appearance is silvery green with clusters of bell-shaped pink flowers in spring. Reaching up to twelve inches, it grows best in higher portions of the bog where it is drier as it does well in garden soil that is moist but not necessarily boggy.

ASTILBE SPECIES
Zones 5–10

Several species and numerous cultivars of this plant range from two to four feet tall and have flowers that are white or various shades of red, pink, and lavender. The flower is either a cluster along a stalk or a feathery plume that rises above the attractive, dark green, fernlike foliage. Astilbes need moist garden soil and semishade.

HEMEROCALLIS
Zones 5–10

Daylilies are perhaps the only plant found in nearly every conceivable growing condition from dry to wet, good soil to poor, high elevations to low, east to west, and north to south. Many thousands of cultivars display a range of colors within the yellow and red hues, and bloom times extend from early to late summer. They range in size from several feet tall to miniature. I recommend you plant them throughout the bog.

HOSTA
Zones 5–10

Hostas, like lilies, are nearly indestructible plants. If hostas won't grow in your garden, nothing will. As with daylilies, hostas will take a variety of situations and can be used in both the wet or drier areas of the bog. Plant variegated varieties (there are several) in shadier areas for brightness and bold-leaf types, such as *H. sieboldiana* and *H.* 'Krossa Regal', near blade-leaved plants for dramatic contrasts.

PHALARIS ARUNDINACEA
Zones 4–10

Ribbon grass is a hardy perennial wanting sun and moist or wet soil. The leaves are ribbonlike and white edged with a green strip up the center. It grows from three to five feet tall and is good for adding brightness to the center or rear of the bog.

SALIX PURPUREA 'NANA'

Hardy to Zone 2

Purple osier is an attractive, fairly recent introduction to the nursery trade that grows in moist to wet soil. It will grow to five feet tall and as wide and is heavily clothed in long, blue-green, lance-shaped leaves. Use to the rear of the bog, preferably on a mound where, if it is able to seek moisture as needed, it will do best.

PLANTING THE TUB GARDEN

A properly planted tub garden does not need to have the water recirculated as long as fish or some other mosquito deterrent is employed. The water will remain fresh if a balanced ecosystem is created and fish—by far the preferable deterrent—will prevent any mosquitoes from breeding. An average-sized tub is about two feet across and will sustain and be sustained by several bunches of submersibles, one miniature water lily, and a couple of margin plants or one margin plant and one floater, though floating plants often become overcrowded. One excellent combination could include a single vertical accent of perhaps a miniature cat tail or iris, a papyrus, or a grass, one miniature lily, one creeping or floating, leaved, margin plant, such as floating heart or pennywort, and several bunches of any of the oxygenating, purifying submersibles. Any of the margin plants and submersibles and many of the smaller lilies discussed earlier will do well in the tub garden.

Conversion Chart

INCHES	MILLIMETERS
0.04	1
0.4	10
1	25.4
4	100
10	254

INCHES	CENTIMETERS
$\frac{1}{8}$	0.3
$\frac{1}{4}$	0.6
$\frac{1}{3}$	0.8
$\frac{1}{2}$	1.25
$\frac{2}{3}$	1.7
$\frac{3}{4}$	1.9
1	2.5
1 $\frac{1}{4}$	3.1
1 $\frac{1}{3}$	3.3
1 $\frac{1}{2}$	3.75
1 $\frac{3}{4}$	4.4
2	5
3	7.5
4	10
5	12.5
6	15
7	17.5
8	20
9	22.5
10	25
12	30
15	37.5
18	45
20	50
24	60
30	75
36	90

FEET	METERS
$\frac{1}{4}$	0.08
$\frac{1}{3}$	0.1
$\frac{1}{2}$	0.15
1	0.3
1 $\frac{1}{2}$	0.5
2	0.6
2 $\frac{1}{2}$	0.8
3	0.9
4	1.2
5	1.5
6	1.8
7	2.1
8	2.4
9	2.7
10	3
15	4.5
20	6
25	7.5
30	9
35	10.5
40	12
45	13.5
50	15

USDA Hardiness Zones *Average annual minimum temperatures*

CELSIUS		FAHRENHEIT
Below -46	ZONE 1	Below -50
-46 to -40	ZONE 2	-50 to -40
-40 to -35	ZONE 3	-40 to -30
-35 to -29	ZONE 4	-30 to -20
-29 to -23	ZONE 5	-20 to -10
-23 to -18	ZONE 6	-10 to 0
-18 to -12	ZONE 7	0 to 10
-12 to -7	ZONE 8	10 to 20
-7 to -1	ZONE 9	20 to 30
-1 to 4	ZONE 10	30 to 40
5 and above	ZONE 11	40 and above

Resources

Aquatic Eco-Systems, Inc.
1767 Benbow Court
Apopka, Florida 32703
407/886-3939

Gilberg Perennial Farms
2906 Ossenfort Road
Glencoe, Missouri 63038
314/458-2033

Lilypons Water Gardens
P.O. Box 10
Buckeystown, Maryland 21717
800/723-7667 or 800/999-5459

Maryland Aquatic Nurseries, Inc.
3427 N. Furnace Road
Jarretsville, Maryland 21084
410/557-7615

Matterhorn Nursery, Inc.
227 Summit Park Road
Spring Valley, New York 10977
914/354-5986

Resource Conservation
Technology, Inc.
2633 N. Calvert Street
Baltimore, Maryland 21218
410/366-1146 or 800/477-7724

Slocum Water Gardens
1101 Cypress Gardens Boulevard
Winter Haven, Florida 33884
813/293-7151

Van Ness Water Gardens
2460 N. Euclid Avenue
Upland, California 91784
909/949-7217

Waterford Gardens
74 E. Allendale Road
Saddle River, New Jersey 07458

Directory of Designers

Bibliography

Clarke, Ethne. 1999. *Water Features for Small Gardens*. London: Ward Lock.

Glattstein, Judy. 1994. *Waterscaping: Plants and Ideas for Natural and Created Water Gardens*. Pownal, Vermont: Storey Communications.

Heriteau, Jacqueline, and Charles B. Thomas. 1994. *Water Gardens*. New York: Houghton Mifflin.

Nash, Helen with Steve Stroupe. 1999. *Plants for Water Gardens*. New York: Sterling Publishing.

Sunset Books. 1997. *Water Gardens*. Menlo Park, California: Lane Publishing.

Index